Journey to Infinity

Johannes von Buttlar was born in Berlin in 1940 and comes from an ancient aristocratic family. He went to school in Germany, and studied psychology and philosophy at university. He also studied astronomy and was made a Fellow of the RAS in 1969. Later, he went to Australia where he served in the Australian Armed Forces. He is married to an ex-opera singer and is now consultant for the Institute for Scientific Information, Philadelphia, and is in charge of their Central European office. At present, he lives in a Gothic castle in Germany.

He has written one other book, *Faster than Light* (1972).

Journey to Infinity

Travels in Time

JOHANNES VON BUTTLAR

Translated from the German by
Olga Sieveking

FONTANA/COLLINS

*For Johannes von Guenther,
wheresoever he may be*

First published in West Germany 1973
Published in Great Britain by Neville Spearman Ltd 1975
First issued in Fontana 1976
Copyright © Econ Verlag, GmbH, Vienna and Düsseldorf 1973
Translation Copyright © Neville Spearman Ltd 1975

Made and printed in Great Britain by
William Collins Sons & Co Ltd, Glasgow

Contents

Illustrations

1. Aura of a celandine leaf
2. Cell meiosis
3. The Count de Saint-Germain
4. L. G. Lawrence's apparatus
5. Boundary stone, Mesopotamia, eleventh century BC
6. Six UFOs in formation
7. Fresco, 1335-50, Dečani Monastery, Jugoslavia
8. A quasar

There is, alas, a type of sceptic,
who will deny credibility to anything
that deviates from what seems to him to be normal.
This book is not for him.
André Gide: *The Vatican Cellars*

1. Triumph over Death

Thus do I pass from the dream-world of the senses,
Through death, to true awareness and vitality.
Hugo v. Hofmannsthal

Women grope their way painfully through the doorways of the house, their heads covered with ashes, for their master has died. Faces veiled, clothing dishevelled, they stumble through the streets lamenting, beating their bared breasts. Every member of the household joins in the woeful procession, men and women, all equally distraught, following their dead lord, whose body is being carried away to be embalmed.

The brains will be extracted through the nostrils by means of metal hooks, the abdomen cut open with a flint knife for removal of the entrails. Each of these organs will be deposited for safe keeping, separately from the rest of the body, in canopic jars – stone vases topped with carved human heads.

The corpse will then be meticulously cleansed and steeped in preservatives, a process continuing for many weeks. Thereafter it will be left to dry out for about seventy days, in preparation for the actual embalming, which involves the use of quantities of different ingredients, such as bitumen, resin, and various oils among others.

To ensure that the outlines of the body are exactly maintained, it will be padded with clay, sand, sawdust, and rolls of linen soaked in aromatic substances.

The priest will lay a ceremonial garland over the dead man's face, throw a handful of incense on to a fire, and chant in monotone:

> A victor's crown awaits you;
> Toum, the God, will set it on your brow,

So that you may live through all eternity
In faith and honour, true to the All-Highest . . .

A further lengthy operation follows, during which the body is wrapped in linen cloths and bandages. Thereafter it is enclosed in a series of wooden caskets, each one fitting inside the next; and at last it is laid to rest in a stone sarcophagus.

Egypt, some two thousand years before Christ. According to the beliefs of the ancient Egyptians, man continues on his path of life through all eternity, beyond physical death. Earth and skies are populated by the living, while the dead exist in a Beyond. But in order that the *Ba* – the disembodied soul – may always be able to recover the body it left behind, the physical frame must of necessity be preserved intact; for the material body is regarded as the permanent home of the spirit-body.

An Egyptian papyrus pictures the returning *Ba* as a winged entity hovering above a mummy.

As long as a physical body can be preserved from disintegration for a thousand or more years, the spiritual body will be able to resume its earlier *persona*, and so the mortal frame can re-incarnate.

Today: four thousand years later.

Elof Carlsson, the well-known scientist at the University of California, believes that in the not-far-distant future we shall be able to create an exact replica of someone mummified four thousand years ago, by re-animating the genes from the desiccated tissues of his body.

The nucleus of any fertile egg-cell will be removed, and the nucleus of a cell from that mummy will be substituted for it. The newly-fertilized egg-cell will then be implanted in an appropriate host, which can provide the necessary nutriment. Before long, cell-division will take place. Multiplication will continue for nine months, until a human baby is developed – an exact replica of the Egyptian who died four thousand years ago.

The process was first tried out during the 1960s by the Oxford physiologist John Gurdon. His first experiment was made by isolating nuclei from the cells of a frog's intestines and implanting them in frog-spawn, the nuclei of which had been destroyed by radiation. By this means he succeeded in breeding a number of tadpoles, several of which grew up into perfectly normal frogs.

This proves that every individual cell of a living body contains a 'blue-print' of the entire organism. According to Robert Sinsheimer, the eminent biologist at the California Institute of Technology, the process might actually come to be used with human cells during the present century. In this way, he believes, any number of exact genetic copies of a particular human being could be created.

The discovery of the means whereby characteristics are transmitted began about a hundred years ago at Schloss Tübingen in Germany. Friedrich Miescher, a Swiss scientist researching into the structure of human cells, found that, in addition to carbon, nitrogen and oxygen, the cells contained a hitherto unknown constituent, which he named *nuclein*.

It is in the nucleic acids that our inherited tendencies are stored. They control assimilation and catalysis – and thus the production of albumen. In fact, they influence our entire development.

Each human cell consists of forty-six microscopic units – called chromosomes – except the germ-cells, which contain only twenty-three. Each chromosome that is fertilized is capable of producing a whole new complex. The genes – the smallest transmitters of heredity – are embedded in the chromosomes, and each of the different characteristics is localized in the genes in a particular section of the chromosomes.

In 1924, Robert Feulgen, a physiologist working at Giessen, identified the main constituents of chromosomes – DNS (desoxyribo-nucleic acid). It was not until twenty years later, in 1944, that Oswald Avery, an American, realized that DNS is the chief transmitter of the genetic memory. DNS is, in fact, the key to life as a whole, being responsible for transmission and metabolism, with the help of certain 'emissaries'. These 'messengers' programme the production of enzymes (albumenous matter) in the cells, and the enzymes themselves proceed to build up all the other albumenous molecules required in the body, in addition to what they themselves need.

In 1953 two Englishmen – J. Watson and F. Crick – established the structure of DNS, which is known as the double helix. After X-ray analysis and further immensely detailed work, they managed to build a model, and were awarded a Nobel prize in 1962 for their research.

Basically, the double helix resembles a rope-ladder, the rungs of which are twisted spirally round one-another. They consist of alternate molecules of sugar and phosphate. The rungs of this structure always combine two sugar molecules facing each other, and consist of four different chemicals, the nucleotid bases:

Adenin=A   Cytosin=C
Guanin=G   Thymin=T

The four nucleotids are arranged in a particular sequence along the DNS structure and, in effect, form the blue-print for the complete hereditary information of an organism. Up to the present, the genetic code of some of the lowest forms of life only has been decoded.

The first person to decipher such a genetic 'code', as one might call it, was an American biochemist, Robert W. Holley, who published the results of his investigation in 1965. He had succeeded in isolating and identifying by chemical means seventy-seven different sections of a 'translating medium'.

The 'translator' combines amino acids with the required albumens – in other words, it translates (or interprets) the genetic code into the language of albumens. Since this interpreter is, in fact, the facsimile of a section of the DNS, the whole genetic code could in this way be broken.

In 1967, Arthur Kornberg contrived to synthetize the entire DNS structure of the virus phi X 174.

In 1970 Gobind Khorana, an Indian, created the genes of yeast cells from a number of fragments in a test tube. Only quite recently two American biochemists – H. Temin and D. Baltimore – in collaboration with S. Mizutami, a Japanese, discovered an enzyme of the human organism that is of the greatest genetic importance; for by means of this enzyme the deciphering of the genetic code is enormously simplified. It makes possible the reconstruction of the DNS hereditary substance directly from the 'messenger' in the cells themselves.

Until then it had been supposed that the messenger substance must first copy the code from the DNS structure and then transport it to the albumen production-centres within the cells; in other words, that the genetic code had first to be translated into the 'albumen language' which, if successful, would produce the building blocks (amino acids), and the enzymes would then weld them together.

There are something like a hundred million genes in a human cell, but so far only about a thousand have been isolated. The discovery of this enzyme will certainly make the deciphering of the genetic code very much easier.

The most recent discoveries in biochemistry, moreover, indicate that even ageing and death are programmed in the genetic code; that, in fact, they are *acquired* characteristics of the more highly developed forms of life, and need not of necessity form part of an organism. Might it be that Nature has programmed death, in order that a stronger urge for survival should produce still more potent successors, who would again live, have issue – and die?

Although this enzyme will simplify analysis of the genetic code, a considerable time must elapse before it can be fully 'read'.

Yet, if we progress along these lines, it should not be impossible to re-programme the genetic code so as to prolong life and to postpone natural physical death for a period of time that seems to us at present to be enormous, improbably fantastic. For in that event a man might well reach an age of up to four or six or even eight hundred years in full possession of his mental and physical faculties.

With re-programming, the capacity for renewal in the human organism might be increased and the progress of ageing greatly retarded. Symptoms of degeneration could be eliminated, to give a long, a very long, span of active life.

Just how these possibilities are to be reconciled with the threatened over-population of our planet and the pollution of our environment – not to mention the continually increasing elaboration of our means of destruction – is, of course, another question. Clearly, the solving of these problems must be a matter of primary importance, for there is no sense in prolonging life unless life is really worth living.

Again, the possibilities of genetic manipulation naturally involve dangers. For, when it comes to it, *who* is to decide *what* changes are to be made in *whom*? And *how* will it be decided whether or not such modifications are for the benefit of humanity?

The aim to produce a 'perfect' human being might in certain circumstances turn out disastrously, for even the *concept* of perfection is relative.

Birth, life and death order our being, and in the brief span between coming and going, most of us spend our days in some form of feverish activity, just to keep ourselves alive and to ensure that we make the most of the little snippet of time that Nature allows us here on earth. Even if some of us manage to scrape up enough of this world's goods to be able to cultivate interests that go beyond the mere struggle for existence, it is all too often not until we are on the downward path as regards health and vitality.

Is it to be wondered at that the ancient Egyptians tried by every possible means to make sure of a life beyond death – and that, similarly, modern man does his utmost to make certain of resurrection by more up-to-date methods?

One of the newer of these methods was evolved in the USA. According to this, the dead would be deep-frozen in fluid nitrogen at a temperature of minus 196°C; for changes and reactions in the human frame that take place in one-millionth part of a second at a temperature of 37°C, take a milliard years at minus 196°C.

The idea is to freeze bodies as soon as possible after death in order to preserve them in perfect condition for the day when future scientists will be able to thaw them and bring them back to life.

The pros and cons of this plan have naturally aroused controversy. And Professor C. W. Ettinger, the originator of it, quite realizes that the freezing process itself will, in the present state of our knowledge, cause considerable organic damage.

Meanwhile there are, not only in America but also in Europe, several 'Deep-Freeze Burial Institutions'; and something like a hundred bodies, wrapped in aluminium foil, with a freezing mixture in their veins, lie in deep-frozen, stainless steel coffins, awaiting their eventual reawakening.

Just as it was in ancient Egypt, the decisive factor nowadays is money; this form of prophylaxis is not exactly cheap.

So there they all are: Egyptian, Chinese and South American mummies; men of the Iron Age, preserved until modern times in and by the peat in which they were buried two thousand years ago; and now they are joined by those who lie deep-frozen in this atomic age – the dead who hope to return.

Not a single individual exists in our world who has not returned from the dead. Indeed, we have all died many deaths before coming to this present life. What we call birth is only the correlative aspect of death – a different name for the same process, seen from the opposite viewpoint – just as we refer to the same door, whether we are looking at it from the inside or the outside of a building . . . Is not the body, according to the Buddhist

concept, simply visible, materialized consciousness . . .?
says Lama Govinda in *The Thibetan Book of the Dead*

A hitherto unrecognized form of energy, radiating from
all forms of life, now shows that existence is even more
complex than has hitherto been thought by scientists.

For thousands of years mystics have believed that the
human body is surrounded by an aura and they have
always said that man is enclosed in an envelope of force
invisible to the naked eye. But the existence of the phenomenon was never proved by traditional methods. Since 1939,
however, it has actually been possible to photograph an
aura by means of an apparatus evolved by two Russian
electrical experts, Semyon Kirlian and his wife. These
two were able, by using high-frequency impulses in a
high-tension field, to release a discharge of radiation within
the visible and ultra-violet spectrum, and to record the
results on a photographic plate. By this means it has been
shown that all forms of life have an aura, and from this it
is argued that an aura is in reality a field of energy surrounding every living creature.

In co-operation with the University Alma-Ata, the
Kirlians have, by means of their camera, not only shown
that the aura changes in colour and intensity according to
the state of health or the emotional condition of an organism, but they have also discovered another curious phenomenon. If, for instance, a piece is torn off the leaf of a
living plant, the aura of the missing fragment persists for
a time as a sort of 'ghost'.

The aura does not leave a body completely until after
death has occurred.

Lao-Tse says:

No man is enlightened until he has learnt that death is
inherent in all life, and life in death; nor until he recognizes that every being incarnates at birth and lays aside
the earthly garment in death only to repeat the process
after a period of growth and development, throughout

unnumbered cycles . . . For life here below and in the beyond comes within the sphere of dualism and change, and not of unity that is insusceptible to transition and mutability.

2. The Mysterious Count de Saint-Germain

I am today,
I am yesterday,
I am tomorrow.
As I pass through recurrent births
I am ever young and vigorous. . . .
    Egyptian Book of the Dead

When you come to think of it, it is only natural that we should want to understand the meaning of Time; for life becomes intelligible only by referring it to time – that transitory spell between birth and death – that tragically brief span that barely allows us to fathom our own existence – the progressive advance of death, the trials of ageing which, so scientists tell us, begin even at the moment of conception.

Biochemists nowadays strive as passionately to delay the onset of death, to lengthen life, as in olden times alchemists sought the elixir that would preserve eternal youth.

It is difficult to decide where alchemy really had its origin. Egypt, Greece, and China all have a claim. Alchemists themselves refer it back to Hermes Trismegistos (the thrice-great), whose name derives from the syncretic philosophers of Hellenistic Alexandria and signifies the God of Wisdom, Thoth. Hermes is said to have written a number of treatises on the so-called secret sciences (medicine, the composition of metals, as well as alchemy). The Emerald Table (Tabula Smaragdina), too, is attributed to him. Of these texts only fragments have survived.

It is a fact that metallurgy and the art of healing were taught as esoteric subjects and were considered to have had their source in divine inspiration.

In many respects alchemy represents the foundation of modern chemistry and physics; practical experiments on all kinds of substances have always formed a part of research in the natural sciences. The philosophic side of alchemy, on the other hand, developed more and more along the same lines as Freemasonry, Theosophy, and Rosicrucianism, in aiming at sublimation and purification.

It is often wrongly assumed that the main efforts of alchemists were directed towards the making of gold. This is a mistake. The aim was to refine and purify humanity and all Nature. It was applied impartially to material things, to the cosmos and to man. The changing of base metals into gold was, therefore, regarded as only a *part* of a *general* process of transmuting all that is corruptible into incorruptibility. The immediate purpose meanwhile was to find the panacea, the cure for all ills, the elixir of life.

Whatever one may think about the elixir, it is a remarkable fact that many of the alchemists who were engaged in this work attained to what was for those days an astonishingly great age. The average expectation of life at the time was about thirty-five years. Yet

Albertus Magnus	lived from	1193–1280	87 years
Roger Bacon		1214–1294	80 years
Raymond Lully		1235–1315	80 years
Arnold of Villanova		1240–1313	73 years
Nicholas Flamel		1330–1418	88 years
Bernard of Treviso		1406–1490	84 years
John Dee		1527–1607	80 years
Michael Sendivogius		1566–1646	80 years
Saint-Germain		1651–1896(?)	245 years

It has been proved, too, that they all remained remarkably youthful, mentally and physically, up to the end of their long lives.

The great enigma among them is, of course, the Count de Saint-Germain. Various books of reference describe him simply as an adventurer. The French police in the Century of Enlightenment considered him to be a Prussian spy.

The Prussians thought he was a Russian agent. And the English arrested him as a suspected Jacobite. In 1745 Horace Walpole wrote to a friend in Italy: 'Recently a curious individual known as the Count de Saint-Germain, who has been living here for the past two years, was arrested. He refuses to say where he comes from or who he is, but admits freely that he is living under an assumed name.'

Lord Holderness wrote to the British Ambassador to Prussia: 'Interrogation elicited nothing of importance.'

Certainly the eighteenth century had its sphinx. Here was a man who not only spoke perfect English, Spanish, Portuguese and French, as well as remarkably good German, but was also familiar with the classical languages. In addition, he was a brilliant raconteur, and could tell hitherto unknown details about the lives of Cleopatra, Pontius Pilate, Henry VIII, Mary Tudor, and others.

An immensely rich man, surrounded by an aura of mystery, who could produce diamonds and other precious stones of unusual size and brilliance, and who was able to transmute baser metals into gold.

It was, indeed, his collection of precious stones that brought him into ever-increasing prominence and gave him the reputation of being an alchemist. Baron Charles Henry de Gleichen, for instance, the Danish diplomat, who published his memoirs in Paris in 1813, wrote: '. . . He showed me some remarkable things – a great number of coloured brilliants and other stones of unusual size and perfection. I thought I was seeing the treasures of the fabled Cave of Jewels . . .'

Voltaire, the cynic, and probably the greatest genius of his day, referred to Saint-Germain as 'a man who knows everything and never dies'. And he wrote to Frederick the Great, saying: '. . . I think it quite probable that this man will visit you within the next fifty years.'

Louis XV, too, was fascinated by Saint-Germain, who was presented to him by the Marshal de Belle-Isle in the salon of Madame de Pompadour. The King's mistress described the Count as being aged about fifty, intellectual, cultured, an amazingly gifted conversationalist, his dress simple but in excellent taste. In addition to wearing several splendid diamond rings, he carried a gold snuff box and a watch adorned with similar jewels.

The most astonishing stories were told about his age. So, for instance, a stranger who remarked to Roger, the Count's valet, that his master must have been lying when he said he was four thousand years old, was given the following reply: 'I know better than that. When I first came into his service a hundred years ago, the master told me he was three thousand years old. Perhaps he'd forgotten the odd nine hundred!'

Similar stories were current in Court circles: as, for example, the following, told by Touchard la Fosse in his *Chroniques de l'Oeil de Boeuf*:

'At Versailles the Countess de Gergy recognized Saint-German as being the image of a man whom she had known in Venice fifty years earlier, about 1710, when she was ambassadress there. She asked him if it could have been his father?

' "No, Madame," replied the Count calmly. "I was myself living in Venice towards the end of the last century and in the early part of the present one, and I had the honour of being presented to you at that time."

' "But that is absolutely impossible," the Countess exclaimed. "The man I knew then was about fifty years of age, and I am sure you are younger than that now!"

' "Indeed, Madame, I am very old."

' "But in that case, you would be nearly a hundred!"

' "It is not impossible," replied Saint-Germain.

'He went on to remind the old lady of conversations they had had, and of some of his musical compositions that had pleased her.

' "Are you still unconvinced, Madame?"

' "No, no – say no more – I believe you," she interrupted. ". . . most extraordinary . . ." '

And the Baron de Gleichen, again, notes in his memoirs: '. . . the composer Philippe Rameau (1683–1764), and a relative of the French ambassador to Venice, assured me that they had known Monsieur de Saint-Germain in the early 1700s, when he appeared to be a man of about fifty'.

After 1701, therefore, the life of the Count de Saint-Germain can be traced more or less chronologically.

1743   In London. He lived there, as Horace Walpole tells us, for two years.

1745   He was arrested as a Jacobite. His personal description: of medium height and colouring, exceptionally cultured.

1745/48   He was one of the most popular persons at the Viennese Court.

1749   At the invitation of the Marshal de Belle-Isle, he made his first appearance in Paris.

1756   He met Sir Robert Clive, administrator of British colonial rule in India.

1758   Back again in France. At Versailles Madame de Hausset, lady-in-waiting to Madame de Pompadour, described him as being aged about fifty.

1760   Commissioned by Louis XV, he went to The Hague to help settle the sensational peace treaty between Prussia and Austria. This, incidentally, seriously displeased Choiseul, the French Minister for Foreign Affairs, who accused him of treason and wished him to be consigned to the Bastille. The Dutch were, however, enchanted with him and refused to agree to his extradition. He fled to England, and the *London Chronicle* produced an article concerned particularly with his 'eternal youth' . . . 'No one now doubts it, although at first it was thought to be pure fantasy. In fact, everyone believes that, among other things, he knows of a panacea for all diseases and is able to overcome old age.'

1762   Took part in the deposition of Peter III of Russia, and in bringing Catherine the Great to the throne.

1763   Carried out further experiments in his laboratory at the Castle of Chambord, which Louis XV had put at his disposal in 1758.

1768   Turned up in Berlin.

1769　He appeared in Italy and established a factory in Venice in which a new kind of silky material was made from flax. During the same period he was also reported to be a sculptor.

1770　He was seen in the uniform of a Russian General with Prince Alexei Orloff in Leghorn. The Orloff brothers frequently referred to the important part he played in the 'palace revolution'. During the next few years he, together with his friend and pupil, the Landgrave of Hesse-Cassel, carried out chemical experiments and studied Freemasonry and Rosicrucianism.

1774　His presence is noted at Schloss Triersberg with the Markgrave Karl Alexander of Ansbach; while staying here, he called himself by the alternative name of Count Welldone (Weldon).

1776　In Hamburg.

1777　Reported to be in Leipzig.

1779　Princess Amalie of Prussia, the sister of Frederick the Great, met and became interested in him.

Between 1776 and 1779 he is said to have offered Frederick the Great a number of chemical formulae, which would have put Prussia in the forefront of the Industrial Revolution if the King had been interested. Mesmer (1734–1815) said that Saint-Germain had explained the subconscious mind to him (thereby preparing the way for modern psychology and psychiatry).

1780　A piece of violin music, said to have been composed by Saint-Germain, was published in London by Walsh.

1784　He was back again in Germany and said to be staying in the castle of the Landgrave of Hesse-Cassel. While the Landgrave was absent from home on one occasion, Saint-Germain is reported to have died, attended only by two women servants. A contemporary entry in the Church register at Eckernförde states that the 'so-called Count of Saint-Germain and Weldon' died on 27th February, and was buried privately. No other details are given.

1785 An important congress of Freemasons was held in Paris. Among those present were Rosicrucians, Kabbalists, Illuminati, and members of other secret societies. It is quite clear from the Masonic archives that, among many others, Mesmer, Lavater, Saint-Martin, and also Saint-Germain attended, and that the latter addressed the meeting. He is also said to have been received by Catherine the Great during this year.

1793 The story goes that Saint-Germain appeared to Mamade du Barry on the scaffold; and to Marie Antoinette in prison, to warn her of the exact date and time of her execution.

1821 Madame de Genlis, the educationist, mentioned in her memoirs a conversation she had had with Saint-Germain during the Vienna peace-talks. And in the same year the French ambassador, the Count de Chalon, spoke with him in St Mark's Square in Venice.

1842 Saint-Germain is mentioned in connection with Lord Lytton, whose close friend he is understood to have been, and whom he is said to have helped to develop supernormal powers.

1867 A meeting of the Grand Lodge of Freemasons was held in Milan, and was attended by Saint-Germain.

1896 Mrs Annie Besant, the theosophist, wrote that she had met Saint-Germain.

Throughout the years, Saint-Germain frequently amazed his contemporaries by describing such things as locomotives and steamships, which had not even been invented at the time. And rumours that he possessed the Alchemists' Stone and that he had drunk of the Fountain of Youth were never-ending.

There is no doubt whatsoever that he was a member of the Rosicrucian Society. It has even been suggested that he was himself the founder of the fraternity, Christian

Rosenkreuz; that he knew the Hermetic secret, whereby he had become immortal; and that, in the course of history, he re-appeared over and over again under various aliases.

Saint-Germain himself claimed that he was four thousand years old, and that he owed it to having discovered the elixir of life.

According to the evidence of the witnesses quoted above, the Count is said to have been about fifty years old in 1701, so that by 1821 he would have reached the positively biblical age of 170. In 1896 he would have been 245 years old – a life-span that seems absolutely fantastic at the present day, when the average expectation of life is about seventy years. How much more fantastic must it have appeared at a time when the average expectation of life was about thirty-five.

Today, only a single document is known to exist that can with certainty be attributed to Saint-Germain. It is kept in the Library at Troyes and, in addition to symbolic drawings, it contains a mysterious text. The following extract must have had a particular significance for Saint-Germain: 'We moved through space at a speed that can be compared with nothing but itself.

'Within a fraction of a second the plains below us were out of sight, and the earth had become a faint nebula. I was carried up, and I travelled through the empyrean for an incalculable time at an immeasurable height. Heavenly bodies revolved, and worlds vanished below me. . . .'

Saint-Germain's real identity will probably always remain a mystery. Perhaps he was a secret agent . . . Perhaps he was the prototype of all the tricksters of all time . . . Perhaps he was what he claimed to be – an adventurer in the realms of Time . . . Perhaps, some day, we may know more.

3. A Door into the Unknown

Do as you please.
For where spirits have entered
Even a philosopher is welcome.
He will raise you a dozen more –
To prove his art and his good will.
Goethe: Faust II

At all times, from the very earliest days, humanity has been torn between curiosity and fear when confronted with the unknown. Although the 'way across' is alluring, uncertainty, dread and prejudice still keep the door into the mysteries closed.

Quite unquestionably, another world exists beside our every-day, visible universe; a world in which space and time have meanings different from those with which we are familiar, another dimension, from which every now and then the Unknown reaches across to us, arousing wonder or terror.

This does not fit into our matter-of-fact world, or so one would suppose. Yet a multitude of well-authenticated cases, some of which are quoted here, go to prove the contrary.

The following adventure befell a scientist, whose integrity is beyond question, and who is well known to the present writer. This is the story as he told it:

Some years ago I was in Australia, the last place where one would expect to meet with this kind of experience; for Australia is, and always has been, a country of pioneers, and life is spent mainly in the open air – a new world, in which metaphysical adventures would hardly seem to have a part.

The date was 1957, and I was studying at Melbourne University. The vacation had just begun, and I was fruit-picking on a large estate in the Dandenong Hills with one of my fellow-students, a Chinese, named Ang. We had been doing this for a fortnight, and I had got heartily sick of it. So, considerably sooner than I had originally planned, I boarded a train in Dandenong and returned to Melbourne. Ang stayed on.

My only problem now was to find lodgings, because I had given up the room I had lived in during the previous term. I soon found what I wanted among the advertisements in a newspaper – a place in East Melbourne that sounded convenient.

It was a blazing hot day, and I strolled towards East Melbourne past Flinder Street Station and through the park.

Some of the most delightful houses are to be found thereabouts, surrounded by large, well-kept gardens. I soon reached the street in which that room was to be let, and had visions of myself living in one of those elegant mansions. Alas, I was to be sadly disappointed. 'My' house turned out to be shabby and squalid – a mean, grey box of a place, absolutely out of keeping with its environment. I ought to have turned back and left then and there.

Yet something utterly inexplicable seemed positively to force me towards the house; it drove me up the cement steps leading to an open door that had once, long ago, been painted dark green, but whose colour was now flaking off.

I was conscious of a musty, cheerless air as I knocked hesitantly at the door.

I must emphasize once again that some queer effluence which I simply could not resist emanated from that house.

I knocked a second time. Then I heard a movement inside and someone stumped heavily down the stairs. Not until this 'someone' reached the bottom step did I see that it was a woman who stood in the dim entrance – a fat, squat woman, with a dull, expressionless face, and greasy, strained-back hair.

She stared at me out of small, sharp eyes, and then introduced herself as the landlady. I gave her to understand that I was interested in the room she had advertised, intentionally using that word 'interested', because up to that moment I still believed I might get away. However, as far as she was concerned, the matter was settled. She preceded me upstairs to show me the room.

Near the top of the stairs, on the first floor, was an open door. As we went past, I noticed a large double bed with a scruffy, pallid man lying on the bare mattress and rolled in a couple of blankets. Half a dozen children, whom he alternately shouted at and cuffed, rampaged around him. This man proved to be the landlord.

We passed two closed doors. The landlady threw open a third, as though she were about to usher me into a state apartment in a palace. She motioned me into an empty room whose faded yellow walls faced me with an air of weary resignation. Not even a curtain screened the dust-begrimed windows. The only piece of furniture was a bed.

Of course I ought to have turned and left immediately. I had absolutely no reason for taking this room; there were plenty of better ones to be found in Melbourne. Instead, I silently pressed four pounds into the landlady's fat, sweaty hand, shut the door after her, and proceeded to 'settle in' to my new quarters – that is to say, I took a few books out of my suit-case, for there could be no question of actually unpacking. I bolted the door, although I am not usually nervous; then I lay down and began to read. The book was Balzac's *Père Goriot*, as I remember to this day.

Ten minutes or so later there was a knock at the door. Who on earth could it be? None of my friends – thank Heaven – knew that I was here.

I opened the door and found myself confronted by a small swarthy man, who breathed beer all over me. He explained in guttural tones that he was my next-door neighbour, and that he was an immigrant from Poland. This, it appeared, was reason enough for him to slap me on the shoulder and burst into tears. At the same time he proffered a bottle of beer. 'Have a drink,' said he. 'I'm a shift-worker at the brewery, and I get it free.' His nonworking shifts, so he told me, were spent at the race course, winning or losing as the case might be. Tears again poured from his eyes – although this particular day must have been a lucky one, for his pockets were bulging with pound notes. He insisted that I should come and see his room. He at least had a few pieces of furniture: cases of beer stood around in every direction, and a dozen or so salami sausages hung on a string stretched between two of the walls. After another bottle of beer I managed to get away.

Hardly five minutes passed before there was another knock. My first reaction was: for Heaven's sake, not Wadjislav again! And I opened the door rather reluctantly. To my surprise, my next visitor was a big, haggard man, with red eyelids drooping over bleary eyes. 'Well, chum, how's things?' he greeted me, speaking with a rich Australian twang. 'I live two doors farther along the passage; my name is Charles.' The word 'Charles' was pronounced in the most refined 'Oxford voice', which was startling.

'You must come and meet my Sheila,' he invited. In Australia, Sheila is not only a feminine name, but is also a general term for any girl-friend.

What could I do? I followed Charles, imagining that I was about to see a tall, slender damsel, wearing a white frock and one of those fashionable broad-brimmed summer hats, sitting demurely on a chair, awaiting Charles's return.

Very different was the grotesque reality. When Charles opened the door, I saw Sheila perched on the bed like a melancholy cockatoo with a crest of red curls and draped in Charles's pyjama jacket. The over-generous make-up round her light blue eyes had melted and was running down her face in black streaks.

Charles, too, led an unfurnished existence, so we all sat on the bed. It transpired that Sheila was the local prostitute, and that she was interested in philosophy. As we sat there, she suddenly propounded the question: did we really exist or were we perhaps only dreaming that we were alive? And she looked at me with a thoughtful, anxious gaze. Charles lost his temper completely over Sheila's unexpected incursion into metaphysics, boxed her ears viciously, and growled: '*That'll* show you that we *do* exist!' I slipped away unobtrusively during the subsequent rumpus.

For the next few days I spent most of my time reading uninterruptedly. When I was hungry, I had to go down to the kitchen, a repellent hovel, with an uncurtained window facing on to the wall of the next-door house. In the middle of the floor stood a large, greasy table, and against one wall was an ancient gas-cooker; completing the furnishings were several small cupboards, one for each lodger. An unshaded electric light bulb, dimmed by exhalations from the frying-pans, provided a minimum of illumination. Dingy green paint further emphasized the unfriendly atmosphere. There was an all-pervading smell of fish and burnt sausages. At the far end, opposite the entrance to the kitchen, a small, narrow door led to what I assumed was the service cupboard.

Every now and then I used to meet Charles or Wadjislav down there, when we did our cooking, bachelor fashion.

Some four or five days later I suddenly felt an urge to do some drawing. I went out and bought coloured crayons, paper and other necessaries. Having no table in my room, I had to pin the drawing-paper to the wall.

That afternoon I was sketching the figure of a man, whose right hand was clenched, while the left was supposed to suggest a question. But I simply could not get the left hand to give the impression I wanted it to. So I abandoned that and drew a lot of symbols round the figure – trees, snakes, coffins, inverted swastikas, circles, church-windows. . . .

The sun was setting and the light was poor.

For once, the house was quiet. Charles and Wadjislav were out, and by way of a change the landlady and her husband were not quarrelling.

I worked feverishly, but I simply could not finish off that left hand. The evening was growing darker now, but I still went on trying. Then suddenly, for no explicable reason, I took the drawing off the wall and carried it down into the kitchen.

It was darker still there. So I pinned up my paper beside the window, in order to make the most of the last glimmers of light.

There was complete silence.

I stood in front of my picture, straining my eyes to see it.

Suddenly I heard a slight sound. And, without turning round, I was aware that the little back door had been opened. I was not in the least perturbed, and went on staring at my drawing. – Then I noticed something faintly rustling, approaching me. Someone, breathing asthmatically, stopped behind me.

I stiffened.

'You should put some shading there and there,' said a deep feminine voice.

As though hypnotized, I followed her directions – and all at once the hand took shape.

'The snake symbolizes *ananta* – eternity. The man's head represents *brahmarandra* – the crown of the head, the highest purpose. And the questioning hand is the *vama marga* – the left-hand path.' She went on to explain that the way of *ananda* is the ultimate source and generator of all existence, of spiritual bliss. I had unconsciously chosen yoga symbols.

But I turned round in annoyance when I heard her say: 'So you have come at last – I have been waiting for you. Now I can give it all to you, for you have been chosen by *adhyaksa*.' That was really more than I could stomach.

However, my irritation evaporated when I saw before me a slight, middle-aged woman, with very bright dark eyes, and dark hair gathered into a knot, framing a small, intelligent face.

She was wearing a brown-checked tweed tailor-made suit.

Saying no more, she turned and moved back towards the little door that I had thought led to the service cupboard. She opened the door, and I swear there was no light behind it as she passed through.

I waited tensely, motionless, in a sort of blue-green haze, for darkness had meanwhile fallen. – A few moments later the door was re-opened, and the little figure came towards me, stooping under the weight of a stack of books. – Utterly dumbfounded, I took the pile from her. She turned back again towards the door and said something of which I caught only a part: '. . . when you have finished with them, you must pass them on to the right person.' She disappeared. The latch of the door clicked into place.

For quite a while I stood motionless, unable to collect myself.

At last I carried the books up to my room, slipped them on to the bed, and switched on the light.

I was staggered to find that they proved to be immensely valuable old treatises on yoga, bound manuscripts, written in English. The introduction stated that they were intended for certain selected individuals in the West, and were not to be sold.

I read and re-read those books, all night through; I could not put them down. And, though it may sound theatrical, I can only say that my eyes were opened; I discovered secrets, the like of which I never found again in any of the works on yoga that I acquired later.

Next morning at about eight, utterly exhausted, I laid them down and, as I did so, someone knocked at the door. It was Ang, my Chinese student friend.

'How *can* you stay in such a ghastly hole?' he asked indignantly. 'I looked for you all over the place before I managed to track you down. You'd better come straight back with me.'

Quite unaccountably, I suddenly felt that I was free again and could leave the house; I was no longer a prisoner.

My belongings were soon packed up.

'I'm moving,' I said to the landlady as I was leaving. 'You can keep the rest of the money I paid you. – Oh, by the way, who is the woman living in the room behind the kitchen?'

'What woman? Which room?' the landlady looked startled.

'I mean behind the little door in the kitchen. I suppose it leads to the room where that lady lives?'

'But you know perfectly well that that's where we keep brushes and brooms and things.' And she went away, shaking her head.

I left the house with Ang, and never went back.

That all happened years ago and when I think about it today, I know that it really was the service cupboard.

Besides, the lady in question was wearing quite the wrong kind of clothes for Australia. People do not wear tweed suits there, especially on a hot summer's day.

And furthermore – although that only occurred to me later – she spoke with a strong Scottish accent.

And the yoga books? – I handed them on to the right person in due course. Of that I am certain.

Baron Joseph von Eichendorff was born in 1788 at Lubo-witz Castle, near Ratibor in Upper Silesia, and spent his early years there. On one of the near-by estates lived his friend, a young Count. During the winter months, some of the young gentlemen of the neighbourhood used to meet for social evenings at one or other of their homes. On such occasions the conversation often turned to the ghost that was believed to haunt the Count's place; until one day he proposed that they should try to get to the bottom of the matter at one of their next meetings. This took place on a stormy evening.

Shortly before midnight they left the panelled dining-hall and walked through long, gloomy passages to the staircase that led to the upper storeys. Beside the foot of the stairs was a high doorway studded with iron that, so the Count assured them, had not been opened by any human hand for a hundred years. Nevertheless, it was said that once in a while the door *was* opened at night during the winter, and a slender female figure crossed the threshold, ran lightly up the stairs, and vanished above.

It might be worth waiting to see whether anything would happen this evening, the Count suggested.

The young men stood in a group between the staircase and the great door, chatting quietly by the light of a branched candlestick carried by a footman who happened to have been newly engaged on that same day.

Eichendorff, who was leaning against the door, suddenly felt it give behind him. A slight feminine figure, wearing a grey dress and a veil that concealed her face, emerged in full view of them all, turned towards the stairs and ran up them.

The new man-servant, who had heard nothing of the story, followed quickly and lighted her up the stairs. At a point where the flight branched, the man turned to the left, but a white hand motioned him to the right. He obeyed her indication and both vanished from the sight of the watchers.

Suddenly a ghastly shriek echoed through the building, and the flickering candle-light was swallowed up in utter blackness. The young men at the foot of the stairs were horror-struck. Eichendorff was the first to recover. He groped his way through the darkness back to the dining-hall and fetched another of the lighted candelabra. Together with his friend, he rushed up the stairs.

At the top lay the footman, dead. His face was contorted with terror; his right hand still grasped the candlestick. They carried the body downstairs, and as soon as they reached the bottom the door closed of itself.

This story was repeated over and over again by Theodor Storm, and he always added that Joseph von Eichendorff had sworn that it was absolutely true.

Prince Louis Ferdinand of Prussia was killed at the battle of Saalfeld on 10th October 1806.

Karl von Nostitz, his adjutant, told the story:

On the evening before the battle, all the General Staff officers were gathered in one of the rooms at Rudolstadt

Castle, awaiting the return of the Prince, who had left that morning to receive battle orders from the Duke of Brunswick.

At about eight o'clock the sound of horses entering the courtyard was heard.

'Time for dinner, gentlemen,' said the Prince. 'I have splendid news for you! Hostilities begin tomorrow, and we shall have the honour of exchanging the first shots with the French. . . .'

After dinner the Prince was in excellent spirits. Every now and then he went and strummed a few notes on the grand piano.

I was beside him. 'My dear Nostitz,' he said, turning towards me, 'how happy I am at this moment! . . . At last our ship is to weigh anchor . . .'

The castle clock struck midnight. As the final stroke sounded, the Prince's expression changed in an extraordinary way. His finely-cut features turned a waxen colour, and his fingers, as they glided over the keys, stiffened as though with cramp. He passed his hand over his eyes, looked at me, snatched up a candle, rushed to the door and disappeared.

I followed him in dismay along the lengthy passage, the only exit from which was through a small side-door that led to the courtyard. The Prince was outside.

Holding the flickering candle in his hand, he was running with stiff, awkward gait in pursuit of a shining white-veiled figure that moved slowly towards the end of the passage and there vanished.

I knew that there was no door at that end. But the Prince quested doggedly in case there might be some secret opening.

When I caught up with him, the Prince exclaimed excitedly: 'Nostitz, did you see her?'

'Yes,' I answered quietly. 'I saw a woman dressed all in white, whom Your Highness . . .'

'So it was not a dream,' he interrupted, 'I really saw her . . . it was the White Lady!'

I wanted to make sure that the Prince had not suffered

from hallucination, and ran to enquire of the sentry on guard.

To my question the man replied that someone in a white cloak had gone by him and that he had allowed him to pass, thinking that it was a Saxon officer; and in any case he had not had orders to stop any officer. That settled every doubt.

The Prince ordered that the matter was to be treated as top secret. The following morning he mounted his horse. The Infantry was already at Schwarza, and the Artillery was drawn up behind Saalfeld. Louis Ferdinand took his place at the head of his riflemen, who cheered him enthusiastically. Women stood beside the road, in tears.

I followed directly behind the Prince. We passed a slight mound and I observed a strange figure, draped in white. It was not surprising to see women weeping at the prospect of a battle.

The reaction of the Prince was therefore the more astonishing. He reined in his horse, turned and looked at me, and gasped: 'Nostitz! – it's the woman again! ... I'm being haunted by the White Lady!' And he galloped away.

I was not able to investigate the matter then and there, because my horse bolted in the confusion. When I got it under control again, I rode back to the spot where we had seen the veiled woman. It was empty.

I asked the soldiers whether they had seen her. One said that they had seen a good many women weeping. But another answered: 'Yes, Lieutenant, but she hadn't taken much trouble over her appearance! I suppose she had got straight out of bed and had just picked up a sheet . . . Anyway, she's gone . . . I expect she was ashamed to be seen in her night things . . .'

Prince Louis Ferdinand was killed during the battle, and his adjutant Karl von Nostitz was badly wounded.

This story is told by Dr Hans Wahl, *Prince Louis Ferdinand von Preussen* (published in Weimar, 1917).

Similar stories are told all over the world – one might

almost say that pretty well every one of us has at one time or another met a ghost story. – The simplest thing is to shrug it off as nonsense. But that would be too easy, because there are so many reliable witnesses. And, as Schopenhauer put it: 'Every issue passes through three stages before it is admitted to be true: In the first stage it seems absurd; in the second it is sniped at, in the third it is regarded as obvious.'

If these phenomena are really not to be looked upon as hallucinations, how are they to be explained? Is there a life after death? If so, do such visions originate in the kingdom of the dead? And, if they do, why do they appear in 'our' world?

Do they sometimes come to warn us of danger? Or are they emissaries from a kind of reception committee in another dimension?

In these days many scientists are fairly certain that every form of life has, in addition to its physical body, a second, normally invisible energy-body (the astral body). It is to be assumed that this unknown energy-body outlasts physical decay, clinical death.

In these circumstances it might be supposed that such visions, which are usually described as shining white or phosphorescent, are the energy-bodies of the dead, which are in some cases seen even before death.

East Grinstead, Summer 1970.

Mr Richard tells the story:

We had spent the week-end with our friends Dick and Moira Aldridge at their country house. After a late supper on the Sunday evening, we were sitting beside a fire in a large room with three french windows leading across a terrace into the garden.

Although the day had been hot and we had spent the greater part of the afternoon in a swimming-pool, the air had cooled down after sunset. So the fire diffused a pleasant warmth in that room, whose walls were panelled with slabs of sandstone.

Conversation was desultory, as often happens when one relaxes in a comfortable chair after a lazy day.

Only my nephew Chris and Tony, the son of the house, were carrying on a lively discussion about their last cricket match; both attend the same public school.

It was a quiet night, no wind, not a sound came from outside.

Suddenly all the doors of the french windows flew open, and a violent gust of wind swept through the room.

Dick stood up and went out on to the terrace.

'Odd – not a leaf is stirring outside,' he muttered, shaking his head. 'Well, perhaps there's a thunderstorm brewing.' And he closed the windows again.

Valerie, my wife, had gone on talking quietly with Moira. Dick and I sipped our drinks without saying anything.

Once again the doors burst open. This time we all sat up. Dick went outside once more, and came back looking puzzled.

'I don't understand it; it's absolutely calm, there isn't a breath of air.'

He could think of no explanation of what had happened. Again he shut the windows.

Meanwhile, the time was coming up to half past one, and we had to think of moving, because only the two boys were on holiday. We had just stood up to say our farewells, when two of the windows were blown open for a third time by a howling blast. And outside we saw a shadowy white figure, that faded slowly as the wind died away.

'Did you see it too?' Chris asked me falteringly.

I only nodded. Except for Dick, who was standing with his back to the window, we had all seen it.

We drove home thoughtfully. Next morning Dick rang us up. His neighbour, Mr Dellinger, whom we also knew, had died at about a quarter to one, after a long illness.

Apparitions from another world do not always portend death. At times, indeed, they appear quite mysteriously from the Unknown to bring succour, as the following incident shows:

In 1828 Robert Bruce, a Scot aged about thirty, was working as helmsman on a merchant vessel sailing between Liverpool and St John in New Brunswick. One day, when the ship was not far from the coast of Newfoundland, he was busy in his cabin, which was next door to the captain's, plotting the course.

He was not altogether satisfied with the result, and called out to the captain, whom he thought he could see over his shoulder sitting and writing in his own cabin: 'What do you think about it, sir?'

Getting no reply, he went over. But when the man at the desk raised his head, Bruce realized that he was facing a complete stranger.

He ran up on deck and told the captain. Both hurried below, only to find that the captain's cabin was empty. But on his slate stood the words in an unknown handwriting: 'Steer north-west'.

All aboard who could write were made to give a specimen of their handwriting – but none resembled that on the slate. Even the search for a stowaway produced no result. – However, the captain decided to steer north-west – at worst, it would only mean the loss of a few hours' time. And before long a ship in distress was sighted, a wreck, completely ice-bound, on its way to Quebec. Death would have been certain for passengers and crew.

When the shipwrecked company was brought aboard, Bruce saw among them one who was the very spit of the man he had seen writing in the captain's cabin. He started back in amazement, and the captain asked the stranger to write the words 'Steer north-west' on the back of his slate. It was the same handwriting as that on the other side.

The captain of the wrecked vessel said that the writer had fallen into a deep sleep at about mid-day, and had said when he awoke: 'We shall be saved today.' – The man had told him how he dreamt that he was on board a ship that would rescue them. When this ship actually hove in sight, the captain had recognized it immediately from the accuracy of the description. And the writer himself declared that he recognized everything on board; he had seen it so clearly in his dream.

(Retold from *Footfalls on the Boundary of Another World* by R. Dale Owen, former American envoy to Naples. Publ. Philadelphia, 1860)

It has often been said that at the moment of death people appear to their relatives or close friends, usually in a dream. But every now and then someone appears at this time in so realistic a form that it is not until later that the one to whom the vision is granted knows that anything out of the ordinary has happened.

A classic example of this is the McConnell case. Lieutenant David McConnell was a British airman in the First World War. He had been eighteen years old when he joined up, and was now about to be promoted. On the morning of 7th December 1918 he was unexpectedly ordered by his commanding officer to fly a Sopwith Camel aircraft from the air base at Scampton to Tadcaster, some sixty miles distant.

At 11.30 he said goodbye to his room-mate, Lieut. Larkin, and told him that, because he was ferrying an aircraft to Tadcaster, he would not be able to attend machine-gun practice that day. But he thought he would be back by tea-time.

Another pilot accompanied him in a two-seater aircraft, to bring him back to Scampton after he had completed his mission.

They set out in good flying weather. But as they approached Doncaster it got foggy and they landed to ask for further instructions. McConnell was told to use his own judgment. – They took off again. The fog thickened, and the escort aircraft made a forced landing, while McConnell continued on his way to Tadcaster.

He reached his target, went down in a crash-landing and hit the ground with his propeller foremost. He was hurled forward and struck his head on the machine-gun in front of him.

A young woman who had seen the crash tried to come to his assistance, but found him already dead. His watch had stopped at exactly 15.25 hours.

The funeral took place four days later. At the ceremony, Lieut. Hillman, another member of the unit, told McConnell's father that at the time of the crash McConnell's room-mate had seen him. The father wrote to Larkin immediately and received a reply on 22nd December, in which Larkin told him that, on the afternoon of the day on which McConnell had flown to Tadcaster he, Larkin, had been sitting in front of the fire, reading and smoking. – He had heard steps coming down the passage, and then the sounds that usually heralded McConnell – who thereupon walked in.

He heard McConnell say: 'Hullo, boy', and turned half round towards the door, which was about eight feet from where he was sitting. McConnell stood in the doorway with one hand on the door knob, smiling. He was wearing his pilot's uniform, but instead of the regulation headgear he had on a sailor's cap – which he used to wear at times, because he was very proud of having been a member of the Royal Navy Air Service.

'Hullo, back already?' said Larkin.

The figure whom he believed to be McConnell replied: 'Yes, I got there all right. Had a good flight.'

And, after a pause: '. . . Well, cheerio', and he went out, closing the door.

Shortly afterwards, at 15.45, Lieut. Garner Smith entered and said he hoped McConnell would get back in good time, so that they might go out that evening. Larkin replied that McConnell was back already and had just been in the room.

Larkin was certain that he had seen the vision between 15.15 and 15.30. And Garner Smith confirmed that it had been 15.45 hours when Larkin told him that McConnell had just been there.

McConnell's appearance had been so life-like that Larkin took it to be real at the time. It was not until the evening that he heard about the crash. At first he had been so convinced of McConnell's physical presence, that he assumed that McConnell had for some reason returned and then taken off again. He could think of no other explanation. As a sceptic about metaphysical phenomena, he was only too anxious to persuade himself that he had not seen McConnell; but he knew that in fact he had seen him.

(From *Psychical Research Today* by D. J. West)

One strange happening after another could be quoted, proving that, in addition to our every-day life with its physical limitations, another, utterly unfathomable world exists, with other laws and a different 'reality', inconceivable to us.

It may be that what we regard as our life is no more than a brief interlude in the true reality of a conscious existence before birth and after death – an existence that is part of a universal pool of percipience or world-consciousness, in which everything that has ever happened or that is going to happen is already recorded.

'Man,' said Paracelsus, 'has two bodies – the material and the astral – and these two bodies form a single individual. Death sunders the two bodies from one another. Similarly, there are two souls in every man, the eternal and the natural. The one is subject to death, the other prevails over it. Thus, what man is, is concealed and no one sees him as he really is, which is revealed only by his actions. During sleep, while the material body is resting, the astral body is active, for it does not rest during sleep. But while the material body is awake and operative, the astral body rests.'

4. Hypnotic Experiments in Time

How wonderful are they
Who interpret the inexplicable,
Read what was never written,
Disentangle what is confused
And find a way through everlasting darkness.
                    Hugo von Hofmannsthal

'You are tired – very tired. Your eyes are closed and heavy. – You are completely relaxed – totally relaxed and weary. You are thinking of nothing – just listening to my voice – my voice soothes you. – You are perfectly relaxed and very tired. – You are going to sleep – deeper and deeper – deep, dark sleep – deep, dark, quiet sleep – deep sleep – no ordinary sleep – a deep – soothing – deep, hypnotic sleep – you are thinking of nothing – hearing only my voice, nothing but my voice – and falling ever deeper asleep – deeper and deeper asleep – you are sound asleep – asleep – you are now in a deep – a very deep sleep.

'Now we are going back in time – back forty-two years. Today is the 14th January 1929. – What is your name?'

The hypnotist looks expectantly at the middle-aged woman lying on the couch with eyes closed.

'Mary Anne Hansome.'

'And how old are you, Mary Anne?'

'I'm nine!' A note of pride in the youthful voice.

'Tell me, do you know what day of the week it is?'

'Yes – it's Monday.'

'What have you been doing today?'

'Well – first I went to school.'

'And then – what did you do next?'

'Then I did some painting.'

'Very good. – But now we're going back even farther. Three years farther back. It's the 4th August 1926. – Now, how old are you?'

'Six.'

'And what is your name?'

'Annie.'

'Do you know what day it is today?'

'Wednesday?' says an uncertain childish voice, and a shy smile appears on the woman's face.

'And what have you been doing today?'

'I cut my finger!' At the same time the sleeping woman points the index finger of her right hand at the hypnotist.

'How did that happen?'

'Oh – there was some glass.'

'Where was the glass?'

'Don't you know?'

'No – you tell me!'

'It was while I was picking up shells.'

'Oh – you were collecting shells, were you? Where did you find them?'

'On the beach, of course – you *are* silly!'

'Right, Annie. – But now we're going back even farther in time – back another three years. – This is the 4th January 1923. – What is your name?' The hypnotist's voice is intent.

Silence.

'Come now – tell me what your name is, won't you?'

'Annie.'

'And how old are you, Annie?'

A short pause – and then she awkwardly stretches three fingers towards the hypnotist.

'And what day is today?' The hypnotist looks at the woman expectantly.

No reply. She twiddles her fingers nervously.

Then: 'Fed [Fred] keeps on taking my Teddy . . .'

'And what have you been doing today, Annie?'

'He's always taking my Teddy!'

'All right. But now we'll go farther back again – another three years back. – What is your name?' A penetrating look at the sleeping figure. But she only purses her lips and babbles in incomprehensible baby-talk.

'And now we'll go back still farther in time – back to

before you were born. It is 1913.'

The hypnotist looks at his patient watchfully. A remarkable change comes over her. The babyish expression has vanished from her face. She breathes deeply and regularly.

'What is your name?' The hypnotist's voice shows suppressed excitement.

'It is light – quite light.' The woman's voice sounds normal, but a long way off.

'Tell me who you are!'

'I am floating – floating,' and the voice fades away.

'That will do.' The hypnotist's voice breaks off, but he looks concerned. 'You are in a deep, restful sleep. – Now we'll go forward in time – quite slowly, one step at a time. – Well, now it's 1971 again, and you are fifty-two years old. You are feeling perfectly quiet and relaxed, and you are simply listening to my voice. What is your name?'

'I am Mrs Warden.'

'How old are you, Mrs Warden?'

'I am fifty-two years old.'

'Right. Now you are slowly waking up – and when I snap my fingers you will be fully awake – rested and relaxed. Now – you are awake.'

Experiments of this kind have often been carried out. Several sessions are usually needed before it is possible to reach a state of hypnosis deep enough to make a regression in time feasible.

At a first glance it must seem astonishing that long-forgotten memories of childhood rise to the surface so readily under hypnosis – things that one would never think of in normal circumstances. But it must be remembered that the subconscious can be unlocked by hypnosis.

The human mind has very often, and quite rightly, been likened to an iceberg, whose tip projects above the water and represents normal consciousness. The much larger part that lies below the surface represents the subconscious. Here, in the depths of the mind, all the forgotten details of our past are stored up. C. G. Jung, discussing the collective unconscious, was convinced that we all carry in us memories that go back to the very beginning of human existence.

Under hypnosis many people recall astonishing things about former lives, and thereby give some reason to believe that a part of us survives death and will be born again. If this is true, memories of former lives must exist in every one of us.

The only problem is to differentiate between genuine memories of past lives and forgotten details of the present span.

If, for example, someone 'remembers' under hypnosis that she was a needlewoman in the Middle Ages, it cannot be said with absolute certainty that she may not accidentally be identifying herself with a character in some book that she has read and forgotten.

On the other hand, how is one to explain that a woman, who is not musical and has never so much as touched an instrument, suddenly proves able to play the organ extremely well under hypnosis? In this condition she remembers a previous life, when she lived in a small town in a foreign country and was an organist; she even speaks the language that was current in that country at that time.

If one accepts the possibility of re-incarnation, one must also admit that the mind is more than a result of bio-chemical reactions in our brain cells. And this is where difficulties begin. Does an 'I am' exist independently of the brain? Do we exist solely through the functioning of our physical organism? If that were the case, all the evidence proceeding from a great number of extremely well-authenticated investigations, which show that the human mind can triumph over matter, would have to be rejected.

Furthermore, how is it to be explained that operations in which part of the brain is removed do not cause mental disturbance? An odd story is told about the autopsy on a well-known architect, Karl Friedrich Schinkel, who died very suddenly. Immediately prior to death he was completely conscious. His skull was found to be empty except for the membranes covering the brain, as Berthold C. Beneke, the eminent anatomist, told his students in Berlin.

Equally noteworthy is the fact that, in many cases, the mentally ill, most of whose life has been spent in mental darkness, suddenly become perfectly 'normal' at the approach of death.

So far, then, we have discovered that, under hypnosis, Mrs Warden re-lived various stages of her childhood. And not only that, but her mentality apparently adjusted itself automatically to the point at which it would have been at the different ages. She spoke like a nine-year-old, a six-year-old, a child of three, and in the end behaved like an infant. Yet, as soon as she went back beyond her birth, she again spoke with the understanding of an adult.

It seems as though the spirit must slowly grow accustomed to the drawbacks and limitations of the body. It must gradually re-learn how to move the body, to speak only through the mouth in order to make itself understood by physical means.

How active and receptive the mind of a new-born child really is can best be illuminated by the following experiment. Dr K. Lyons, a Boston psychologist, had hypnotized Loulie, the fifteen-year-old daughter of Marcia Moore, a well-known teacher of yoga, and had returned her to her fourth birthday. Loulie remembered the birthday party. After this, Dr Lyons took her farther back into the past, to events of which she had normally not the smallest recollection.

In her trance, Loulie saw lights, and a number of people busily engaged in a room in which she was herself, near her mother. It proved that she had re-lived her own birth, for her mother confirmed that she too remembered the bright lights and bustle in the hospital ward.

One of the most widely-publicized cases of hypnotic regression to an earlier life is that of Virginia Burns Tighe. Virginia Burns Tighe was born in 1923 at Madison, Wisconsin, in the USA. Her father, George Burns, divorced her mother very early, and so Virginia was from the age of three brought up by an aunt, Mrs Myrtle Grung, in Chicago.

After a perfectly normal childhood, Virginia spent a year and a half at the North-Western University, and then married. Her husband was killed in the Second World War. She moved to Denver and there met Brian Tighe, who became her second husband. Subsequently Brian and Virginia Tighe lived in Pueblo with their three children.

By chance, the Tighes made the acquaintance there of a successful and intelligent business man named Morey Bernstein. After being present at a hypnotic session, Bernstein had become interested in trance phenomena, and he took up the study of hypnotism in addition to his regular career. He studied therapeutic hypnosis, became an amateur hypnotist, and worked with qualified doctors in a number of medical cases. He was attracted particularly to problems of parapsychological phenomena, which he began to investigate in depth.

He came to the conclusion that work on parapsychology led quite naturally to the question of re-incarnation. Proof was, it is true, to be obtained only by chancing upon a suitable individual whom he could conduct into an earlier life through hypnosis.

Several attempts had by this time shown that Virginia Tighe, being exceptionally sensitive and herself interested in hypnosis, was particularly well suited to help in such an investigation.

When she had gone into a deep trance, she replied to questions, at first about her immediate childhood. Then, when Bernstein transferred her back into the past before her birth, she spoke about Ireland. Virginia Tighe said she was Bridey Kathleen Murphy, the daughter of Duncan Murphy, a Protestant lawyer, and his wife Kathleen, and that she was born in Cork in 1798. She referred to her brother, Duncan Blane Murphy, and to a second brother who had died in childhood. She talked about her school, the head of which was a Mrs Strayne, and of Aimée Strayne, her daughter, who married her (Bridey's) brother Duncan.

She herself had at the age of twenty married, in a Protestant church, Sean Brian Joseph McCarthy, the son of a Catholic lawyer. Bridey and her husband had moved to Belfast, where Brian had attended classes. Later Brian, as Virginia (Bridey) told in her trance, had taught at Queen's University. A second, Catholic, marriage service had been celebrated by Fr. John Joseph Gorman in St Theresa's Church. Bridey and Brian had been childless, and in 1864 Bridey had died and been buried in Belfast. In her trance she used the word 'ditched' for 'buried', about which there was some argument.

Neither Virginia Burns Tighe nor her husband had ever been in Ireland. Many things of which Virginia spoke under hypnosis could not normally have been known to her, especially local dialect expressions, which were subsequently identified by language historians as having been current at that time.

A book that caused a considerable sensation was published under the title *The Search for Bridey Murphy*. Articles appeared, and discussions 'for' and 'against' led to unpleasantness that obliged Virginia and her family to leave Pueblo for the sake of peace and quiet. The most violent attacks from *Life* and *American* followed, in which every attempt was made to discredit Virginia and to convict her of making false statements. These difficulties were, however, easily disposed of.

An 'iron bedstead', off which Virginia said she had scratched the paint as a child, would not, according to *Life*, have existed at the time. But Dr E. J. Dingwall, a British historian, proved that newspaper advertisements for metal bedsteads had been published in 1830 by The Hive Ironworks of Cork. Virginia Tighe's statements, recorded on tapes, were very indistinct and in parts difficult to follow. This led to misunderstandings, as was shown when tapes were re-played.

According to the researches of William J. Barker, editor and reporter on the *Denver Post*, it transpired that certain expressions such as *tup* (a vulgar word for any male person), *linen* (for handkerchief), *brate* (small cup), were still in common use in Cork in 1880.

Bridey claimed to have read *The Sorrows of Deirdre*. This was disputed by *Life*, because Synge had not published the book until 1905. But Barker showed that a small volume by Bolton had been published in 1808, under the title *The Sorrows of Deirdre and the Death of the Sons of Usnach*.

One way or another, most of the statements made by Virginia Burns Tighe under hypnosis were checked and found to be accurate and in keeping with Bridey Murphy's life.

For instance, she mentioned the names of the only two food shops in the neighbourhood at the time of her (Bridey's) death – Farr's and Carrigan's. She referred to coins in use at the time, among them a twopenny piece – a coin that was in circulation only between 1795 and 1850. The Queen's University did of course exist; it was founded in Belfast in 1850.

The expression she used for burial ('ditched') was identified by Professor Seamus Kavanaugh, head of the Linguistic Department at the University of Cork, as being in general use between 1854 and 1856, after the great famine, as a synonym for 'to bury'.

Since no population census was taken in Ireland until 1864, neither the name of Bridey Murphy nor that of her husband could be found in any public records and although someone named John McCarthy was mentioned as working at the Queen's University, it could not be proved that this was in fact Bridey's husband.

Dr Lyons was at first also among those who disputed the case of Virginia Tighe/Bridey Murphy but subsequently he admitted it as an authentic proof of regression.

That excellent journalist Jess Stearn was another who, like Dr Lyons, was interested in regression. He invited the well-known hypnotist, Joseph Lampl, founder of the Academy of Applied Mental Sciences in New York, to accompany him to Canada to investigate a case.

In Orilla, Ontario, lived a seventeen-year-old girl, Joanne

McIver, who was believed to have lived before. Lampl hoped to be able to take her back under hypnosis to an earlier life.

Lampl hypnotized Joanne, and led her back to her life as Susan Garnier-Marrow. In that life Susan (Joanne) was born in 1832. Her father was a farmer, and she remembered the names of various neighbours. She recalled her marriage to Thomas Marrow, also a farmer, and his death as the result of an accident on the farm, after which Susan had led a wretched existence as a young widow, living in a lonely hovel.

Jess Stearn wrote saying 'how greatly he was impressed by the accuracy with which so young a girl reproduced details of the life of Susan Garnier-Marrow'.

In the very first attempt at hypnosis (by her father), Joanne McIver had become ten-year-old Susan Garnier, hiding in her father's orchard, and watching her brother making love to his sweetheart. Under hypnosis by Lampl, her facial expressions changed noticeably. Oddly slanting eyes blazed in a haggard face, as though another body belonged to this different psyche.

While under hypnosis, she replied to Lampl's questions by giving the exact prices at which all kinds of food and other goods were sold a hundred years ago. Her vocal tone took on a particular rhythm, which allowed her audience to infer her French-Canadian origin in the former life. Susan Garnier-Marrow died in 1903, and under hypnosis she (Joanne) described her own burial, and the actual place of her interment, behind a church. Nowadays, she said, there was a large Army tank training ground on that spot, surrounded by a fence. Joanne's statement was correct. The piece of ground had been transferred to the Army before the Second World War, before Joanne's birth. In response to their application and in view of the special circumstances, Jess Stearn, Dr Lampl, and Joanne McIver were given permission to visit the ground. A Major Malone undertook to act as guide, and soon Joanne was arguing with him about the site of the cemetery and of the church of which she had spoken during her trance.

The Major referred to assurances given to the local population who had moved from the neighbourhood at the time, and produced official plans and maps to prove that neither church nor graveyard had occupied the spot indicated by Joanne.

But, undaunted, Joanne explored the site, and did in fact find fragments of old gravestones under heaps of rubble, and identified the place where the church had formerly stood.

It is not always necessary to have to resort to hypnotism, however, to awaken memories of a past life. There are plenty of cases in which knowledge of a former life needs no great impetus to bring it to the fore. Children, especially, often remember details and events that go back beyond their birth.

Little Imad Elawar, aged two, was walking with his aunt along the village street of Kornayel in Lebanon, when they saw a stranger approaching. The boy ran to meet him and threw his arms round him. Obviously surprised, the man said: 'Why! Do you know me?' 'Yes,' replied the child, 'you used to be my neighbour.'

Imad Elawar was born in 1958 at Kornayel, near Beirut. His first intelligible words were 'Jamila' and 'Mahmoud'. But none of his relatives answered to these names. As soon as he could speak properly, he talked about the beautiful Jamila and compared her critically with his mother. He often repeated the names and told of things that his parents could not make head nor tail of. He spoke of a man who had died as the result of losing both legs when he was run over by a lorry.

Imad insisted that he belonged to a family named Bouhamzy living in Khriby, a village some 18 or 19 miles from Kornayel, that could be reached from there only by crossing a mountain pass. Imad often repeated how glad he was that he could walk, and kept on pestering his parents to take him to Khriby, until it got badly on his father's nerves.

To this day descendants of the Druses live in some of the villages of Israel, Syria and the Lebanon; re-incarnation is one of the tenets of this Islamic sect. So Imad's parents must have known what the boy was talking about. But in the end the child's continual nagging came to be too much for his father, who promised him a good hiding if he didn't stop his 'damned lies'.

After this threat, Imad told no one except his mother and his grandparents about his former life.

But when it turned out that the stranger whom the boy had embraced came from Khriby, the father began to have second thoughts.

The parents had not paid any particular attention to Imad's tales, and had certainly never thought of making any enquiries. They made up their own minds about the names mentioned by Imad, and decided that the boy believed he had been Mahmoud Bouhamzy and that Jamila was his wife.

In December 1963 Imad's father took the boy, now aged five, to Khriby for the first time. No attempt was made to contact the Bouhamzys during this visit.

In mid-March 1964, Professor Ian Stevenson, former head of the psychiatric department of Virginia University, came to Kornayel. A young Lebanese of his acquaintance had sent a letter written in Arabic, introducing Professor Stevenson to his brother in Khriby, and asking him to help the Professor in his search for cases of re-incarnation. Unfortunately the addressee had moved to Beirut.

When Professor Stevenson mentioned the reason for his visit, he was told about Imad Elawar. Of course the Professor immediately proposed taking Imad to visit Khriby. And now it was found that all the names the boy had mentioned were correct. Some of the people were actually still living. Saïd Bouhamzy really had been run over in 1943 and had had both legs broken. He had died after an operation. The rest of the stories did not fit Saïd's life, not even the house to which Imad had so often referred.

But everything fitted an Ibrahim Bouhamzy, the cousin and friend of Saïd, who had lived only a 100 yards away

from him. Jamila had been Ibrahim's very beautiful girl-
friend, with whom – to the scandal of the village – he had
lived in free love. In 1949 Ibrahim had died of tuberculosis
at the age of twenty-five. What had troubled him most
during his illness was that for the last six months he had
been bed-ridden and unable to walk. He had complained
bitterly about this.

One of Ibrahim's uncles was named Mahmoud. Like
his cousin Saïd, Ibrahim had also been a lorry-driver and
had been involved in accidents. All the names that little
Imad had mentioned were connected with Ibrahim's family;
and the stranger whom the child had embraced in the street
had been Ibrahim's neighbour.

On 19th March, Professor Stevenson, together with
Imad and his father, visited the house that had belonged
to Ibrahim and that had stood empty since his death. It
was opened specially for the occasion. Imad knew the
whole lay-out and was able to give correct answers to
questions about what it had been like at the time of
Ibrahim's death.

From where did he get his knowledge? Certain similarities
of character between Imad and Ibrahim were also noted.
The latter's passion for hunting corresponded with the
interest shown by the five-year-old for everything connected
with the chase. Imad spoke remarkably good French for
one of his age, although his own family had no linguistic
gifts whatever. Ibrahim had served in the French army
and had spoken fluent French. Both were quarrelsome and
lacking in self-control. And, during the whole of his present
life, Imad had been terrified of lorries and buses.

Since dreams are always taken to be a source of information about the subconscious, research into dreams might
be expected to produce revealing information about re-
incarnation. Unfortunately only a minority of people are
interested in their own dreams or attribute any particular
meaning to them; unusual aspects of dreams, therefore,
hardly ever attract attention.

Freud's psychoanalytical interpretation of dreams is not sufficient in itself. It is quite indubitable that dreams have a significance apart from this. There is no question but that dreams make us travellers in Time. They are the key to a (for want of a better word) disembodied existence.

One of the most remarkable cases of re-incarnation was investigated in minute detail by the British psychologist, Dr Arthur Guirdham. His patient, known as 'Mrs Smith', often transferred into an earlier life in the thirteenth century, mainly in dreams, but at times also during waking hours.

Dr Guirdham, a sceptic by nature and trained as a doctor and psychiatrist to keep imagination and reality in separate compartments, took the greatest trouble over this case.

In checking Mrs Smith's statements he confined himself mainly to the role of amateur historian, and took no active part as psychologist.

He consulted men of international status, such as Professor Nelli of Toulouse University, and finally, after meticulous investigation of the facts, reached the conclusion that this was a genuine and verifiable case of re-incarnation. This woman had been a heretic in the thirteenth century. She described events, names of places, historical details and the dress of the period, and much else about the time.

Dr Guirdham succeeded not only in discovering the exact date at which she had been denounced to the Inquisition seven hundred years ago, but also the names of her family and of her collaborators. After lengthy and painstaking research, and study by well-known historians, her statements were finally corroborated and attested as correct.

5. The Future in Dreams

It is highly probable that proof of an immaterial, intangible part of our being, extending beyond birth, death and rebirth, is buried in our subconscious, if not indeed indissolubly incorporated in it.

The secret hidden behind human life is illustrated by an extraordinary case that is at present mystifying French psychologists and parapsychologists. It concerns Philippe Levuelle, a four-year-old boy from Marseilles, who suddenly developed supersensory faculties, after having undergone an extremely critical operation by Dr Charles Tallreux. Since this operation, Philippe has been living what might be termed a double life.

He was playing in front of his parents' house near the harbour at Marseilles, when his little friend Jean called to him from the other side of the road to come over. Philippe dashed straight across without looking, was run into by a lorry and dragged for several yards along the street. Despite almost fatal injuries, the doctors, led by Dr Tallreux, succeeded in bringing him back to life, after an operation lasting for two and a quarter hours.

Two months later, when he was back at home, he complained of a pain in his throat. It appeared that an injury to his larynx had been overlooked, and the child had to go back on to the operating-table for a second time. It was a difficult operation, as the doctor told the parents. Part of the larynx had to be removed and replaced by an artificial cartilage. All went well at first, but then difficulties arose. The boy's heart stopped beating; the operation had to be interrupted.

Clinically, Philippe was dead. Nevertheless, Dr Tallreux's efforts at resuscitation succeeded in bringing him back to life. Unfortunately he was not successful at the first attempt, and was obliged to repeat the process another five times.

At last, after four hours, the operation was completed,

and Dr Tallreux, in a state of exhaustion, told the parents: 'It's a success. But if I ever have another operation like it, I shall go out of my mind.'

Three weeks later, Philippe was well enough to leave hospital. But he had undergone an odd change psychically. Not only his parents, but the doctors and nurses at the hospital noticed it. He was much too quiet and serious for his age.

One day the child asked his sister whether she had ever been dead, explaining that he had been dead several times, but Dr Tallreux had always brought him back to life. 'It isn't nice being dead,' he said. 'Everything's so dark and there's such a lot of noise, and queer faces keep staring at you.' How did a four-year-old child know that he had been dead several times? Nobody had talked to him about it.

His parents asked the advice of Dr Tallreux, who at once called in a colleague from the psychiatric department. In conversation with the boy, this latter discovered that the child knew all about his operation, and remembered even the remarks made by doctors and nurses while it was in progress.

As time went on, the parents discovered that he had developed some quite uncanny faculties. One day, as they were on their way to a farm, where Philippe used to go and ride, he suddenly asked out of the blue: 'Is Dr Tallreux going to the farm too?' When his mother asked what made him think that, he said: 'Because Dr Tallreux is driving along behind us.' His mother tried to tell him that he was talking nonsense, but the boy insisted that he knew Dr Tallreux was there. At the next traffic lights, the doctor's car stopped beside theirs. And at the same time Philippe said: 'Oh, now I know. Dr Tallreux is going to collect his girl-friend to go swimming.' He was right.

On another occasion, the boy insisted that he must go at once to see the doctor, to comfort him, because something dreadful had happened. In the end, his parents yielded, and they met the doctor as he was leaving the hospital in a great state of depression. An operation had gone wrong. Philippe had jumped up from his game in tears at the moment when the doctor had realized what had happened.

'Ever since his operation, when Dr Tallreux saved his life, the boy seems to be in such close, unconscious contact with him that he shares his whole life,' said a Paris psychologist. One day the parents were startled by a nerve-shattering shriek coming from Philippe's bedroom. The boy was sobbing and complained that he had got a terrible pain in his right shoulder; and at the same time he kept on saying how sorry he was for Dr Tallreux. When they failed to pacify him, they finally telephoned the doctor. The doctor realized from what the mother said that the boy had burst into tears at the moment when he himself had seriously injured his right shoulder. He was in severe pain, which the child was evidently also suffering, telepathically.

On another occasion, Dr Tallreux was involved in a motor accident and broke his left hand. This time Philippe was visiting an aunt near Marseilles with his parents. Once again the child was in great distress, complaining that his left hand hurt so badly; it was hours before he recovered.

At Dr Tallreux's suggestion, Philippe has been put under the care of several psychologists and parapsychologists, and it is hoped that in time his supra-normal faculties will disappear.

This case shows clearly that a sort of extra consciousness must be present in the human spirit, that can link his fate with another's.

There is plenty of evidence to show that the mind can project itself in time and space through the present and the past. The same can be shown to be true for the future.

It may appear paradoxical that things that have not yet happened can be foreseen. Yet history tells that in the past belief in prophecies of future events played a great part. Dreams have always held a key position in this connection.

The Gilgamesh epic of ancient Babylon, some four thousand years old, probably contains the oldest stories that have come down to us of dreams and their interpretations:

Ere ever you came from the mountain
Gilgamesh dreamt of you in Uruk.

Gilgamesh arose, spoke to his mother,
And told his dream:
'O mother, in the dream that I had this night,
I went fearlessly among the soldiery;
I was filled with power.
The stars of heaven gathered round me —
I was overwhelmed, as by the armoury of Anu;
I would have lifted what fell, but it was too heavy
    for me;
I would have moved it, but I could not.
All the people of Uruk pressed around,
The men kissed his feet;
I leaned upon it, they supported me.
And I raised it and brought it to you.'

The mother of Gilgamesh, to whom all things are
    known, spoke to Gilgamesh, saying:
'It may be, Gilgamesh, that one like you was born
    in the steppes,
And grew up among the mountains. —
When you see him, you will be joyful;
Vassals kiss his feet.
You will embrace him and bring him to me.
It is Engidu, the mighty one,
A comrade who will always help his friend in need.
The mightiest in the land is he, he has power,
His strength is as the strength of Anu.
You lay on him as on a woman
... and he will always keep you safely.'

He lay down to sleep and dreamt another dream;
And to his mother he spoke:
'O mother, I dreamt another dream;
... I sought; in the market-place of Uruk
Lay an axe, men gathered around it,
The people thronged about it:
The axe affected me strangely.

When I saw it, I rejoiced,
I loved it; I lay on it;
As on a woman, I lay on it.
I took it up and laid it at my side.'

The mother of Gilgamesh, wise, all-knowing,
Spoke to her son,
She, Ninssun, wise, knowing all things,
Spoke to Gilgamesh:
'The axe you saw is a man.
You will speak gently to him, as to a woman,
And I shall cherish him as I cherish you.
He will come to you,
The comrade who will always help his friend when
    needed.
His strength is as the strength of Anu.'

And again Gilgamesh spoke to his mother:
'May it come to pass as Enlil, the great Counsellor
    commands.
May I win a friend, a counsellor,
Yea, may I win a friend, a counsellor!'
So Gilgamesh told his dreams.

And Gilgamesh's dreams came true. As his mother had
prophesied, he met Engidu, who had been born in the
steppes, and they became close friends.

The curious thing is – or perhaps it is not – that the
interpretation of the dream given by Gilgamesh's mother
coincides in many respects with modern psychoanalytical
ideas. For example, she takes the axe to be a male symbol;
and followers of Freud would probably explain it as a
phallic symbol.

The Greeks believed that there were two worlds of
equal significance: a rational, logical world of solid objects
and a second, anomalous world that existed in an eerie
darkness and was given over to daemons. This Dionysian
world would also conjure up the dead. It is true that to

the Greek mind, the Dionysian world was closely involved with every-day affairs; and in the main the Greeks considered dreams to be revelations from the gods and heralds of coming events, good and bad.

Many of their dreams spread alarm and despondency. For instance Pan, the goat-footed, horned god, was the bringer of nightmares. The temples of Poseidon played a very important part. Before setting sail, mariners would spend a night in the temple of the sea-god, praying him to send a prophetic dream about the outcome of the venture.

The temples of the god of healing, Asklepios (Aesculapius), too, were of particular significance, for in them the faithful dreamt of curative drugs. Indeed, these dreams became the basis of Greek medicine. Stories of successful remedies, with descriptions of the relevant diseases, were cut into the walls of the temples. In the course of centuries, therefore, an impressive number of therapeutic dreams was recorded, that could confidently be used for curative purposes. Hippocrates' knowledge of healing, for example, was believed to have been derived from the temple records in Kos, his native town.

There is a story that a woman's dream once saved Athens from a plague. In her dream a dead Scythian appeared, advising her that all streets and alleys in Athens should be sprinkled with wine. The Athenians did according to the woman's dream. The plague was prevented, because the wine acted as disinfectant on the tainted atmosphere.

Everyone, no matter who he might be – statesman, official, general – was sent to discover from dreams how to carry out a task in conformity with the will of the gods, and what would be the outcome of an action. Since the interpretation of dreams was of such moment, a man who was skilled in the art was both highly regarded and highly rewarded. In the second century AD, Artemidoros Daldianos compiled a book on the interpretation of dreams that had a great reputation and was widely read. He was of the opinion that dreams often foreshadow future events, although many dreams contain only symbols that need interpretation. A diviner should know all details before undertaking to give the meaning. If the beginning of a dream seemed unclear, he should begin at the end, and then look for the source. If different people had the same dream, he said, it might not necessarily mean the same thing in all cases, and should be read according to individual circumstances.

Stories of prophetic dreams were continually repeated — is there anyone who does not know the story of Joseph's dream of the seven fat and the seven lean kine, for example? And anyone who has read Plutarch will remember the dream of Caesar's third wife, Calpurnia. In the night before he was killed, she dreamt of his murder. She implored him vainly not to go to the Senate.

Just as Caesar ignored the prophetic dream of his wife and the warnings of the diviners who had foreseen the crime, John F. Kennedy disregarded similar predictions. One among many, Jackie Joyce, the woman representative of an engineering firm, dreamt of the murder of the American President. In December 1960, shortly before he took office, she had a dream in which she foresaw the full details of the President's death three years later. In her dream, she first saw President Eisenhower, making a speech in front of a number of microphones, looking anxious and distressed. While she was still looking at Eisenhower, the scene suddenly changed to what appeared to be a hospital room, in which a man was lying on a narrow table. At first she could not see this man's face clearly, but it gradually took on the lineaments of John F. Kennedy. He lay there, inert, and several people were leaning over the table. Suddenly his face became clearly recognizable. His complexion darkened until it was blood red. In her dream, Jackie Joyce knew with absolute certainty that he had been shot. On the following morning she told her dream to a number of acquaintances, including her chief. All through the day she was haunted by the dream, and was deeply disturbed. But in time the memory of it faded.

When, three years later, she heard about the President's trip to Dallas in Texas, Jackie Joyce's disquiet and the memory of her three-year-old dream returned. She was asleep on the day of the murder, because anxiety had kept her awake all through the previous night. A telephone call roused her. Her employer told her that the President had been murdered. 'Your dream has come true,' he said. She rushed to the television set. Former President Eisenhower's grave, shocked face appeared on the screen. He was holding a conference, surrounded by a battery of microphones.

Similar warning dreams foretold the murder of Abraham Lincoln a hundred years earlier. Lincoln had himself foreseen his death in a dream.

Quite startling parallels between the fate of Lincoln and that of Kennedy were noted by Jess Stearn in *Secrets from the Psychic World*:

. . . both fought for the civil rights of coloured people; both were murdered on a Friday and were protected only by casual security measures; both were killed by a shot in the head, and in both cases the wife was present and witnessed the deed. Kennedy was murdered on the hundredth anniversary of Lincoln's proclamation of emancipation. Just as Lincoln had been warned not to show himself in the theatre, so Kennedy had been warned not to go to Dallas.

And there were other remarkable parallels. Each had a Vice-President named Johnson, who had previously been a member of the Senate; and the second Johnson – Lyndon – was the first Southerner to become President since the first Johnson – Andrew – had become President in the same circumstances. Lincoln's murderer, John Wilkes Booth, was born in the year 1839; Lee Harvey Oswald in 1939. Booth shot Lincoln in a theatre and ran out into a shop; Oswald shot Kennedy from a shop and ran into a theatre. Both were themselves shot and killed before being brought to trial. Lincoln and Kennedy had each lost two children, one before going to the White House and one while in office. Kennedy had a secretary named Lincoln, and Lincoln had one named Kennedy.

To take the parallels further: Andrew Johnson was

born in 1808; Lyndon Johnson in 1908. The names Lyndon Johnson and Andrew Johnson each contain thirteen letters; the names John Wilkes Booth and Lee Harvey Oswald each fifteen. Each President married during the fourth decade of his life a twenty-four-year-old brunette who spoke fluent French. Both Presidents were members of a minority party. Both were elected to Congress in the year '47 of their centuries; each failed in his first nomination as Vice-President in the year '56 of his century, in both cases four years before being nominated President. Both had near relatives who were ambassadors to England: Kennedy's father, Joseph P. Kennedy; and Lincoln's son Robert . . .

In mid-August 1829, a letter was written to *The Times* by Mr H. Tucker, telling of an extraordinary dream which his father-in-law, Mr Williams, who lived in Cornwall, had had on the night of 11th May 1812. Mr Williams had found himself in the lobby of the House of Commons, and had seen a stranger firing at and killing a gentleman as he entered. Upon enquiry, he had learnt that the dead man was Lord Spencer Perceval, the Chancellor of the Exchequer. The same dream, which had shocked him considerably, recurred twice during the same night, and he told it to Mr Tucker and other friends on the following morning, that is to say, on 12th May. It was pointed out to Mr Williams that it was most unlikely that the Chancellor would appear in the Lower House. But in the course of that same morning, news of the Chancellor's murder was published. John Bellingham, a double agent, had shot him, exactly as Mr Williams had dreamt. What particularly surprised Mr Tucker was the accuracy with which Mr Williams had described Lord Spencer Perceval, whom he had never seen, and the House of Commons, which he had never visited.

Dreams – what are dreams? A student of Sigmund Freud once said: 'Dreams do not tell you what is going to happen, but what you are going to do.' It is doubtful whether the author of modern psychoanalysis would have agreed wholly with this statement.

Sigmund Freud gave a course of lectures at Clark University in Worcester, Massachusetts, in which, among other things, he discussed dreams. In his view, the interpretation of dreams is the royal road to an understanding of the subconscious; it forms a sound basis for psychoanalysis, and every student should work on this in order to satisfy himself of its truth. He said, in effect:

If anyone were to ask me how to set about becoming a psychoanalyst, I could only reply: by studying one's own dreams. Hitherto, every opponent of the science has – after a polite disclaimer – either not taken the interpretation into consideration at all, or has dismissed the whole subject with superficial arguments.

It must not be forgotten that our nightly dreams have on the one hand an external similarity and an inner affinity with mental disturbances, though on the other hand they may be compared with perfectly normal waking life. . . .

And now, may I invite you to accompany me on a short trip into the land of dreams and its problems.

In our waking hours we are apt to treat dreams with the same preconceptions with which patients treat their relations with a psychoanalyst. Both will be disregarded and completely forgotten as quickly as possible. Our poor opinion of dreams rests on their doubtful character – even those that are neither nonsensical nor confused – simply because some dreams *are* both absurd and confused. We shrug them off because of the sensuality and extravagance that characterize many of them.

It is well known that the ancients did not share this low opinion of dreams, any more than simple folk in our own day doubt the value of dreams. They too, like the ancients, accept that dreams afford a glimpse into the future. I would agree that it is hardly necessary to fill the gaps in our present knowledge with vague mystical theories. Nor did I ever manage to find anything that proved the prophetic nature of dreams. There are plenty of other interesting things to be said about them.

To the dreamer himself, not all dreams are confused, incomprehensible or aberrant. If the dreams of very young children, say from the age of eighteen months on, are investigated, they will be found to be quite simple and easily explainable. Small children always dream of the fulfilment of desires that have been unfulfilled during the previous day. No great skill in interpretation is required to discover this perfectly natural solution; a child need only be asked about its activities on the day before (the 'dream-day'). It would obviously be the easiest solution if the dreams of adults were as simple to unravel as those of children – as the fulfilment of desires experienced on the day before. And that is, in fact, the case . . .

Moreover, one may say that the analysis of dreams shows clearly how the subconscious (unconscious) uses particular symbols, especially those concerned with sexual impulses. In such cases the symbolism differs from one person to another. At times it appears in typical forms and seems to agree with the symbolism that underlies our myths and legends. It may be that the existence of such myths gives the popular explanation of dreams. . . .

As we have seen, although Sigmund Freud denies the prophetic meaning of dreams, he agrees with some of the other ideas of the ancients, which gave a definite interpretation for certain dream symbols.

Those who agree with Freud, for example, believe that if a woman dreams of a smoking chimney it is a phallic symbol; and a man who dreams of an orange uses this as an image of a woman's breast. Freud regarded dreams as the guardians of sleep. That is to say: our wants appear in disguised form, lest a tender conscience should suffer and the dreamer awake in horror.

There are also, of course, other schools of dream-analysis. But in essentials they all rely on Freudian principles. Thus psychologists agree in the main that dreams are a mixture of sensory impressions, pleasant or disquieting daily happenings, and suppressed desires, all subject to censorship, so that they may not disturb our rest. It is not proposed to dismiss these interpretations out of hand, for undoubtedly a large part of the Freudian teaching meets the case. What is difficult to accept is that that is all there is to dreams.

In defence of psychology, Carl Gustav Jung (1875–1961) must obviously also be called upon. He took a much more profound view of dreams. Jung believed that vast records concerning the human mythos lie buried in the Collective Unconscious. Reaching across the bounds of time and space, they come to the surface in our dreams. And the human instincts form a valuable picture storehouse of memories from the depths of time, which have just as much influence on the fate of each individual as have his own actions.

It has also very often been shown that dreams appear as 'feelers' for future events. Just as they can show visions of the past, so they may also give an inkling of future happenings. The prophetic nature of dreams is often dismissed on the ground that this would imply that the future was already fixed and pre-determined, which would mean that free will and freedom of choice could not exist. It still remains true, however, that one event is likely to be the cause of another – so that we can argue that from a particular happening in the past a particular happening will follow in the future. Or even the reverse: we can argue from something that happens now, what must have happened in the past to cause it. There is, therefore, a direct connection between past and future.

Looked at from this angle, there are limits to our freedom of will and of choice. If we perform an action, we cannot, with the best will in the world, avoid some reaction. Once something has been done, it cannot be undone. If you hit your thumbnail with a hammer, it is not difficult to prophesy that the thumb will be painful, is it! In the same way that dreams go deep into the past, it may be that they lead on to coming events. This may well be because the subconscious knows instinctively what future happening must necessarily follow upon a past or present one.

There is, of course, the other possibility: that events are really pre-determined for the future, and are only waiting to be triggered off by ourselves.

A comparison might be made with a tuning fork. If a tuning fork is sounded, it can start off another one tuned to the same pitch.

As usual, Bishop Josef Lanyi was in Grosswardein on 28th June 1914. (Today this place is the capital of Crisana in Rumania, and lies six kilometres from the Hungarian frontier.)

At about half past three in the morning he was jerked very suddenly out of an intensely vivid dream. He dreamt that his morning post had just arrived, and the top letter had a black border and a seal on it. Having been tutor to the heir to the Austrian throne, he immediately recognized the handwriting and the crest. He opened the letter and at the head of the letter saw a coloured picture of a car in which were seated the clearly recognizable Crown Prince and his wife, with two high-ranking officers facing them. Suddenly, from among the crowd of spectators, two men burst out and fired at the royal couple.

The wording of the letter of which he dreamt was as follows:

My Lord Bishop, dear Dr Lanyi,

I am writing to tell you that my wife and I will today fall victim to political assassination. We ask your earnest prayers, and trust that you will continue to be as devoted to our unfortunate children as you have always been.

With kindest regards,

Archduke Franz.

Bishop Lanyi transcribed the letter at 3.30 that night, and all details remained clearly in his memory. In the morning he told his mother and her maid about it.

The attack upon the Crown Prince and his wife followed upon the dream twelve hours later. And the First World War broke out.

Iserlohn 1849.

No. 46 of the *Iserlohn Chronicle*, dated 7th June 1848, carried the following notice:

> I hear on many sides that I am alleged to be the person who recently spread the senseless rumour that terrible murders and bloodshed would take place on Ascension Day. I hereby declare that I have never thought or said this; and I am prepared to offer a handsome reward to anyone who will inform me of the identity of any individual who has spread this rumour, so that I may prosecute him.
>
> Lips, Coachman, at Letmathe.

On Ascension Day, 17th May 1849, just one year after this notice had appeared in the paper, appalling bloodshed did take place in Iserlohn, at that time the most important town in the old Mark of Westphalia. Within a short time, forty people died and a great many were wounded. The population of Iserlohn had, as in a number of other towns, risen against the absolutist government of the Brandenburg regime. So, on Ascension Day, 1849, Prussian troops moved in. After a peaceful start, Colonel Schrötter, riding at the head of his men, was killed by two shots fired by a sniper. In their fury, the soldiers stormed into the houses, searching for arms and armed men, killing as they went.

The future may also be likened to a landscape containing numerous villages, each of which represents a particular event. Many roads lead to the various places. And although one may freely choose which road to follow, it is impossible to avoid the places that lie along the path chosen. Naturally, there are turnings branching off from whichever road one has decided upon, but these roads always lead to certain other places – or events.

A stag hunt was scheduled to take place on 1st October 1850. As Prince Kraft zu Hohenlohe/Ingelfingen was not feeling well, he sent a refusal and went to bed early on the evening of 30th September. In the middle of the night he suddenly woke from a dream in which he had lost control of his horse, which ran him into a tree, leaving him lying on the ground in the forest with a broken skull. At this point he awoke. With his eyes open, he saw himself lying on the floor at the foot of the bed, his face covered with blood. Hohenlohe sat up in bed, wide awake, and stared incredulously at his effigy lying at the foot of the bed, until it gradually faded out. The room was pitch dark. Though the dream disturbed the Prince, the fact that he *was* disturbed by it, made him even more uncomfortable. After a time, he went to sleep again. Once more he awoke, and saw his double lying bleeding on the floor, and again the vision disappeared after a time. But in the faint light of dawn, he had clearly seen all the furniture of his bedroom.

Despite his uneasiness, he decided that he would after all take part in the hunt – if only to 'rid himself of superstition'. The members of the hunt met at the appointed place, and the Prince told his brother Friederich Wilhelm of his dream-adventure. Both laughed over it.

The hunt started, and the Prince's horse bolted immediately, running wildly into the ever-thickening forest; the Prince's head was dashed against a tree-trunk. He recovered briefly from his faint, and found that he was lying on the ground, that the whole of the right side of his face was torn open, blood was flowing from his eye, he was partially scalped, and his head was broken. His foot must have caught in the stirrup, so that the horse had dragged him along in its wild career.

Prince zu Hohenlohe/Ingelfingen was picked up and carried to his brother's house in Potsdam. He did not regain consciousness until three days later. He asked for a mirror and discovered that, beneath the bandages, his wounds were exactly identical with those he had seen in his dream-waking condition during the night of 30th September to 1st October. (Retold from Part I of *Memoirs of my Life* by General Prince Kraft zu Hohenlohe/Ingelfingen, published 1897)

It is not only violent happenings, involving bloodshed and death, that are foreseen in dreams or visions; at times it may be some quite ordinary, every-day matter. Arthur Schopenhauer, the philosopher (1788–1860), tells the following story in his book entitled *Essays in Clairvoyance and its Concomitants*:

Other, at times quite unimportant, events are dreamt in the most minute detail by some people, of which I have been convinced by an unequivocal experience of my own. I am retelling it here, because it high-lights the inevitability of all that happens, even the most casual things.

One morning I was engaged in writing an important English business letter. When I had finished a third page of it, I accidentally picked up the inkpot instead of the sand-box, and poured it over the letter. The ink dripped from my desk on to the floor.

The maid who came in answer to my bell fetched a pail of water to scrub the floor, so that the stain should not become permanent. While doing so, she said to me: 'I dreamt last night that I'd be cleaning ink stains off the floor.'

To which I: 'I don't believe it!'

She repeated: 'It's true; and when I woke I told the other maid who shares my room.' At that moment the second maid, a girl of about seventeen, happened to come into my study to tell the first one that she was wanted. I got up to meet this second maid and asked:

'What did this girl dream about last night?'

'I don't know.'

'Yes you do – she told you when she woke up this morning.'

The younger maid: 'Oh yes – she dreamt she'd been cleaning stains off your floor.'

I vouch absolutely for the truth of this story, which clearly shows the theorematic nature of dreams. It is remarkable no less for the fact that what the girl dreamt was the result of a totally involuntary action on my part – it had occurred simply as the result of a careless movement of my hand. Yet this action was so strictly necessary and so obviously and inescapably planned that its effect was felt several hours beforehand in someone else's dream-consciousness. This is one of the best examples of the truth of what I have said before: everything that happens, happens of necessity . . .

How clearly events can be foreseen is shown by the following experiment which was carried out under the auspices of Professor W. H. C. Tenhaeff, of Utrecht University. Gerard Croiset, the famous medium, proved it most convincingly on 19th October 1949 at Groningen, two hours before the beginning of a séance. In the course of the experiment he said:

I see a lady, with high-piled hair, sitting in the fourth seat from the left, in the third row. She is about fifty-five years old, and is wearing a slender metal necklet with a pendant. She has a pain in the big toe of her right foot – her shoe's tight. One of her three children is planning to emigrate to America. I see a wall – it must be the wall of a convent. I see a very clear picture: the lady is playing with marbles there, as a child. She has a serious quarrel with a boy.

Two hours later, Croiset's statements were proved true. A lady whom, it was established, he did not know, sat in the seat designated by Croiset and pre-determined for her by fate, and all the details described by Croiset were correct.

In England, in 1927, J. W. Dunne published a much-discussed book that is as up to date now as it was then. Its title: *An Experiment with Time*. This book was the outcome of dream-analyses in which Dunne shows that practically everyone foresees future events in dreams.

True, most of such events are of so trivial a nature that people do not remember them when they actually come to pass. As a rule it is only violent happenings that are consciously connected with previous dreams. Dunne's interest in the phenomenon was aroused when he noticed that it happened in his own dreams. In one place he writes:

In the Spring of 1902 I was in the camp of the sixth Mounted Infantry near the ruins of Lindley in the then Orange Free State. We had just come off trek and mails and news arrived but rarely. There, one night I had an urgent and rather unpleasant dream. I seemed to be standing on high ground – the upper slopes of some spur of a hill or mountain. The ground was of a curious white formation. Here and there in this were little fissures, and from these jets of vapour were spouting from the ground. In my dream I recognized the place as an island of which I had dreamt before – an island which was in imminent peril from a volcano. And when I saw the vapour spouting from the ground I gasped: 'Good Lord! The whole thing is going to *blow up!*' For I had memories of reading about Krakatoa (*a volcanic island in the straits between Sumatra and Java*), where the sea, making its way into the heart of a volcano through a submarine crevice, flashed into steam, and blew the whole mountain to pieces (*the eruption of 1883*).

Forthwith I was seized with a frantic desire to save the four thousand (I knew the number) unsuspecting inhabitants. Obviously there was only one way of doing this, and that was to take them off in ships. There followed a most distressing nightmare, in which I was at a neighbouring island, trying to get the incredulous *French* authorities to despatch vessels of every and any description to remove the inhabitants of the threatened island. I was sent from one official to another and finally woke myself by my own dream exertions, clinging to the heads of a team of horses drawing the carriage of one 'Monsieur le Maire', who was going out to dine and wanted me to return when his office would be open next day. All through the dream the *number* of people in danger obsessed my mind. I repeated it to everyone I met and, at the moment of waking, I was shouting to the Maire: 'Listen! four thousand people will be killed unless –'

I am not certain now when we received our next batch of mail and papers, but when they did come, the *Daily Telegraph* was amongst them and, on opening the centre sheet, this is what met my eyes:

VOLCANO DISASTER
in
MARTINIQUE
Town swept away
AN AVALANCHE OF FLAME
probable loss of over
40,000 lives
British steamer burnt

'One of the most terrible disasters in the annals of the world has befallen the once prosperous town of St Pierre, the commercial capital of the French island of Martinique in the West Indies. At eight o'clock on Thursday morning, the volcano Mont Pelée, which had been quiescent for a century . . .'

There is one remark to be made here: The number of people declared to be killed was not, as I had maintained throughout the dream, four thousand, but forty thousand. I was out by a nought. But when I read the paper, I read, in my haste, that number of 4,000. I did not know it was really 40,000, until I copied out that paragraph fifteen years later.

Dunne is of the opinion that time has more than one dimension, which is the reason for our dreaming of future happenings.

An event may, therefore, already have occurred in one dimension of time, while it is still to come in another dimension. According to this, something may already have taken place in a dream-dimension, while it is yet to come in the time-dimension.

Besides, according to Dunne, a time-dimension is one in which all the events a man experiences seem to follow in a particular sequence – a dimension in which an observer (or his observation) does not move backwards, so as not to disturb the sequence of events.

In the course of time, a great many people have racked their brains over the question of time.

6. Travels in Time

'Scientific people', (said) *the Time Traveller*, *'know very well that Time is only a kind of Space. . . .'*

The Time Machine, H. G. Wells

Ever since man became a rational being, he has speculated about time.

His consciousness of light and darkness, of pain and ease, grief and joy, birth and death, has shown him that he cannot escape from time. He is reminded of the past by his memory; he is bound to consider the future by his need to find shelter and food. Night follows day in an ever-recurrent cycle, one season follows another, one year succeeds another. Calendars were invented in an effort to organize oneself to cope with these constantly renewed periods.

No one was more obsessed with time than the Mayas. They regarded time as a sort of magic circle, that was re-created by the continually recurrent need to fulfil certain duties. Buildings were erected if it seemed right by the calendar, not because they were particularly needed. Life and learning, everything was ordered by their astonishingly accurate calendar and by the stars. To Mayas the most important thing in life was a continually recurrent past. They believed that history repeats itself every 260 years to all eternity. In this way past, present and future formed a perpetually revolving circle.

The Babylonians assumed time to be closely connected with the movements of sun, moon and planets. Life and the fate of men depended upon the heavenly bodies.

The Greeks, the Stoics in particular, believed that time was linked with the fate of the cosmos. Although they expected the universe to perish, they were sure it would come again exactly as it had been, including every living being.

With the advent of Christianity, the conception of linear time was born. The fundamental idea of Christian ideology does not admit of recurrence. Everything is aimed at a particular point – the Last Day, the end of the world.

During the Middle Ages, views about the nature of time were divided. Some believed in cyclic recurrence, others in continual linear progress.

Galileo Galilei (1564–1642), in his *Discussions and Demonstrations concerning two new Branches of Learning*, published in 1638, promoted the theory that time was a geometrically straight line and not a circle.

Isaac Barrow (1630–1677), the English mathematician, regarded time as essentially a mathematical concept, similar in many respects to a straight line: which consists only of length, is alike in all its parts, and may be regarded either as a simple addition of contiguous points or as the unceasing progression of a single point. Furthermore, Barrow believed that, whether anything was in movement or at rest, whether we were awake or asleep, time continued on its uninterrupted course.

And Isaac Newton (1642–1726/7), who followed him, advocated the view that time, like space, is absolute (*Philosophiae Naturalis Principia Mathematica*, published in 1687). In view of its nature, he considered that absolute time was always constant, independent of matter.

Yet even Newton's own Law of Classic Mechanics limited his theory of absolute space and time. If, for example, a steward on an ocean-going liner drops a plate, it will fall to the ground at exactly the same rate as a plate dropped by a waiter in the Hilton Hotel. The fact that the steamer is travelling through the water at speed, while the hotel is firmly fixed to the ground, makes no difference. Within the ship there is nothing to show its movement through the sea (unless you happen to look over the side!).

The theory that time and space are absolute is not, fundamentally, tenable. For it is, in fact, only objects and their physical laws that determine time and space.

Albert Einstein (1879–1955) began to tackle the problems of space and time in 1905. To begin with he tried to bring the electro-magnetic theory of light-waves, put forward by the English physicist James Clerk Maxwell (1831–1879), into accord with the rest of physics, which were based on Newton's mechanics.

When it was discovered that light moves in waves, and that these light-waves had different, measurable lengths and frequencies, a comparison was made between them and sound-waves. Since sound-waves need a medium such as water, air or solid matter through which to move, it was assumed that the same must be true for light-waves. But light-waves will also progress through a vacuum, therefore some such medium must also exist in a vacuum, it was argued. Long and detailed research was carried out to try to trace this medium, which was named 'ether' – but with no result.

In the hope of finding proof of the existence of ether, two American scientists, A. Michelson and E. Morley, measured the speed of light simultaneously in opposite directions in 1887. They were of the opinion that if one ray of light were projected in the same direction as that of the earth round the sun, and the other at right angles to this, the two speeds must be different, if ether existed. But the results were found to be absolutely identical.

Other experiments also showed the speed of light to be constant. The study of binary-star systems in particular confirmed this. Binary stars revolve round a common gravitational centre. While one star is travelling away from us, the other is approaching us. Then they change directions and the first star comes towards us while the second recedes. The point to be noted is that the light of both stars takes the same time to reach the earth, no matter in which direction they are travelling.

According to the latest calculations, light moves at the rate of 2.99793×10^8 metres per second – that is, roughly, 300,000 kilometres per second – in a vacuum. The theory was thus proved that the speed of light is absolutely independent of the speed of the source of the light.

After Einstein had carried out his researches into the problem of ether in 1905, he announced his Special Theory on Relativity. He argued, first, that the existence of ether cannot be proved; and second, that the speed of light relative to the observer is always constant.

In order to explain Einstein's first principle, we may imagine a journey into space. We board a space-ship and leave the earth at a speed of about 50,000 kilometres an hour. The earth is left far behind and we are surrounded by the darkness of interstellar space.

Suddenly a light approaches. Another space-ship catches us up and, as it goes past, a question reaches us over the intercom: 'What's up? Why have you stopped? Has anything gone wrong?'

We know, of course, that our ship is moving, but we cannot prove it.

When the second space-ship has passed us and has vanished in the darkness, it is evident that it must be much faster than ours. Besides, by means of our instruments we can easily calculate that the speed of the other ship is about 10,000 kilometres an hour greater than our own. But that is all. Since our own speed when we left the earth was 50,000 kilometres an hour, we can only assume that the other ship is proceeding through space at 60,000 kilometres an hour, and was therefore catching us up at the rate of 10,000 kilometres an hour. Whether or not that is correct is another question. It would be just as likely that – with reference to the earth – we were moving at the rate of 10,000 kilometres and the other ship at 20,000 kilometres an hour. Or again, it might be that the second ship was standing still while we were going back towards the earth at 10,000 kilometres an hour.

Without some stationary object to which to refer, we should never discover which of us was moving, or in which direction. Even the most sensitive instruments could not help. With the best will in the world, it is impossible to speak of absolute movement, only of movement relative to something else. Even an observer cannot be certain that he is standing still. And it is on the principle that all movement is relative, that Einstein's theory of relativity is based.

Everything in the universe is in motion. The earth turns on its own axis and circles round the sun. The sun moves in relation to the other stars in our galaxy, which itself rotates and moves in relation to other astral systems. Everything, in fact, moves in relation to everything else. There is, therefore, no heavenly body to which we can refer as a fixed point for calculations.

Even if ether were to exist, it could not be verified, for stationary ether would be the only thing without movement in the universe, because it would be in absolute motion. But since only relative motion can be determined, there is no way of proving that ether exists.

To go back to our experiment with the space-ship: it is impossible for anyone inside the vessel to tell whether it is moving or at rest. Nor could anyone judge whether or not the earth is moving through the ether (supposing this to exist).

The following example illustrates Einstein's second and revolutionary theory:

Suppose a police-car is following some bank-robbers at a speed of 100 kilometres per hour. The police officers fire at the tyres of the gangsters' car, and the bullets leave the revolver at also, say, 100 kilometres per hour. Relative to the police, therefore, the bullets travel at a speed of 100 kilometres per hour. But relative to the ground their speed is 200 kilometres per hour because their speed is doubled by the rate at which the car is travelling.

From this it might be argued that light-waves emitted by a source of light approaching us should be faster than those emitted by one retreating from us. But this is not the case, as the Special Theory of Relativity shows.

It is known that light-waves move at a speed of about 300,000 kilometres an hour relative to an observer. Whether the observer and the source of light move towards or away from one another does not affect this in any way. The speed of light remains unaltered.

Newton's mechanics were changed by the theory of relativity. In Newton's view, time and space were two separate principles that led him to conceive of a factual eternity.

The theory of relativity, on the other hand, shows that time and space, like mass and energy, have practical meaning only when considered in relation to one another – and this shows that no single dimension is absolute, but only the totality. The length of an object moving away from an observer at speed appears to diminish in the view of the observer. That is one reason for regarding the speed of light as constant.

To return yet again to the space-ship: both ship A and ship B are 20 metres long. If they are flying side by side at the same speed – in other words, if they are standing still relative to one another – the captains of the two vessels would see that each is 20 metres long. But if ship B were to increase speed to 150,000 kilometres per second (half the speed of light), the captain of space-ship A would decide if he were able to measure it, that space-ship B was only 17 metres long. If space-ship B increased speed again to nine-tenths of the speed of light – that is to say, 270,000 kilometres per second – B would appear to A to be only 10 metres long. Yet to each captain his ship remains unchanged at the same length – 20 metres – whatever his speed. For the observer, an object decreases more and more as it approaches the speed of light, until finally it becomes infinitely small.

It is a fact that a kilometre is shorter at 150,000 kilometres a second than a stationary kilometre – a further reason for agreeing the constancy of the speed of light – since, according to the theory of relativity, there is no such thing as absolute space.

Increase in the mass of an object moving away from an observer is another postulate of Special relativity. That is to say that, as it approaches the speed of light, the mass of, say, a space-ship grows continually more dense as far as the observer is concerned, until its mass becomes infinite when it reaches the speed of light. This has been proved by experiments with electrons flying at speed.

Time, too, is affected by movement, for time passes more slowly for a rapidly moving object. It used to be assumed as a matter of course that time proceeds at the same rate for everything and everywhere in the universe. But this idea too was revised by the theory of relativity. For two observers moving relatively to one another time passes differently.

To go back yet again to the space-ships: if these two fly past each other at high speed, the 'personal time' of the occupants of either space-ship paradoxically passes more rapidly than that of the occupants of the other ship. This fact has also been proved by experiment.

Under natural high radiation there exist so-called mesons (medium-weight, short-lived particles) with a life-span longer than that of similar mesons artificially produced in a laboratory. The explanation for this was discovered only when it was shown that mesons in conditions of high radiation, compared with those produced artificially, more with almost the speed of light. And, by applying the theory of relativity, it was found possible to calculate that, although high-radiation mesons live a hundred times longer when reckoned in 'laboratory time', their own, personal life-span is just as short as that of the slower, artificially produced mesons. The same is true for travellers in the two space-ships passing one another.

A further experiment – a clock paradox – will give another example of how the displacement of time acts. Not long ago two American physicists, J. Hafele and R. Keating, flew round the earth twice in opposite directions – one eastward and the other westward. Armed with four absolutely accurately synchronized atomic clocks, they were determined to get to the bottom of the mystery of time. They found that, after thirteen landings and take-offs, quite a considerable amount of acceleration relative to the earth had taken place.

It turned out that the clocks really did work differently above than on the ground. Going eastward, they 'took it easy' and lost 50 nano-seconds (1 nano-second equals 1 milliardth part of a second). Going westward, they made up for it and gained 140 nano-seconds. Of course, the rotation of the earth also plays its part in this.

Might the result show that the effects of the relativity theory will prove to be to the advantage of future projects in interstellar space-travel? It is quite possible that some day science and technology will be able to solve all problems connected with the construction of a space-ship that is intended to travel at almost the speed of light.

Until that time comes, it may be worth while to take an imaginary trip into the future.

Engineers have developed the 'ram-jet'. This machine is most economical to run, and need carry hardly any fuel – for throughout its journey it will find an ever-ready source of supply – interstellar hydrogen atoms. There will be plenty of these. It has been calculated that there is one atom of hydrogen to every cubic centimetre in interstellar space. To this may be added the accumulation of much denser concentrations in hydrogen clouds – amply sufficient to supply the ram-jet with this rarified gas as it approaches the speed of light.

The ram-jet itself is the centre of an electro-magnetic field, surrounding it in a radius of somewhere between 100 and 1,000 kilometres. During flight, interstellar gas is ionized and diverted to a zone of reaction in or near the ram-jet through the magnetic field. Energy is therefore generated by fusion. The unconverted mass is driven backward by the energy that is released, and thus a recoil is produced. Since this recoil is constant, the necessary speed for interstellar space-travel can be reached.

So now the ram-jet is in position, ready for take-off. Final preparations are complete for the trip to the star Epsilon Eridani, some eleven light-years distant. The average age of the crew is thirty. The astronauts are hoping to find that Epsilon Eridani has a planet on which intelligent life exists.

The ram-jet takes off into the night sky on a glistening beam and is soon lost to sight. By constant acceleration, the space-ship achieves a speed of twenty million kilometres an hour after only a week. And the earth is now over five milliard kilometres distant.

By the end of the eighth month the ram-jet is already flying at two-thirds of the speed of light. And then the astronauts begin to doubt the accuracy of their navigational instruments; for they ascertain that in these eight months they have already covered a quarter of the total distance.

This means that Epsilon Eridani is not eleven light-years distant from earth, but only eight and a quarter. How was it that the distance had added up to eleven light-years?

The astronauts are so confused that they check and re-check their calculations, and immediately discover exactly how far they are from earth. But this only makes their confusion greater. They are not, as they calculate they should be, two and three-quarter light-years away from earth, but only a quarter of the distance they *should* have covered in eight months. Earth is much nearer than expected. The distance they had calculated before the start has actually been diminished by a quarter.

Then the astronauts remember the theory of relativity, according to which space is not absolute. The reduction they have discovered must, therefore, be somehow connected with the speed of the ram-jet in relation to earth and Epsilon Eridani. Since after eight months the ram-jet has reached a speed of two-thirds of the speed of light, the distance is cut by a quarter.

After another four months, during which they constantly accelerate, they are approaching the speed of light; and now space contraction works out in such a way that distances in the cosmos diminish to practically nought.

During the following year the ram-jet's 'brakes' are applied, in the hope of being able to land on one of Epsilon Eridani's (hypothetical) planets.

The entire journey to this star, believed to be eleven light-years distant, has therefore taken only two years – one year in which to increase speed to near the speed of light, and a second year in which to slow down. To their disappointment, the astronauts find no life and turn back immediately towards earth. Once again they increase speed over a year until they approach the speed of light, and then slow down for another year so as to be able to land on the earth.

Over all, they have been absent from home for about four years and are now about thirty-four years old. Happy at the prospect of seeing wife and children again at long last, the astronauts step off the ram-jet. But everything looks different – they recognize nothing, and no one recognizes them. Wife and children have died long since, and their great-great-grandchildren . . . do not know them.

Time passed more slowly in the space-ship, so they profited by the dilation of time in comparison with those who remained on earth – and they have therefore landed in the future on their return. The more nearly a space-ship's speed approaches that of light, the greater will be the difference between earth-time and space-ship-time. Thus an earthly hour in a space-ship moving at 96% of the speed of light becomes the equivalent of seventeen minutes; at 97% it diminishes to fifteen minutes; at 98% it goes down to twelve minutes, and at 99% to six minutes.

Even though these particular astronauts failed to discover any extra-terrestrial life, that does not mean that the chances of doing so are negligible. Just the opposite is true. But it has taken a long time for Science to concede the point.

For at least 1,500 years scientists regarded the earth as the centre of the universe. Then they found themselves obliged to agree that the earth revolves round the sun, which gave them a new centre for the universe. But this idea was tenable only until it was realized that our sun is only one star among many milliards in the Milky Way; and not only that, but that our galaxy is only one among many milliards in the universe.

Our delusion that at least our sun was the central point of the Milky Way, was shattered about fifty years ago by the Harvard astronomer, Harlow Shapley. He reduced our solar system to the position of an unimportant suburb in the Milky Way, something like 30,000 light-years distant from the centre.

Our galaxy is about 80,000×100,000 light-years in extent. It is lentil-shaped, and the existence of spiral ramifications that were for a long time suspected, was not confirmed until radio-astronomy was developed. Our solar system lies on the outer extremity of one of these spirals and revolves round the gallactic centre once in 225 million years. Nowadays it is reasonably certain that among the 150 milliard stars in our Milky Way many have planets that are thought to be surrounded by a zone of moderate temperature (ecosphere) capable of sustaining life. The American astronomer, Peter van de Kamp, investigated sixty of the stars in our neighbourhood for anomalies. Among these sixty, van de Kamp found seven with dark companions – planets. And the Barnard Star, six light-years distant from us, is circled by the smallest of the planets so far discovered – 1.6 times the mass of Jupiter.

Not only planets, however, but also the 'building blocks' for the development of life were discovered in the cosmos. Amino acids, ammoniac, formaldehyde, formic acid, hydrocarbons . . . cyanide acetylene, for example, a substance that contains every essential for developing life, was discovered by radio-astronomers at the Greenbank Observatory, Virginia, in gas-cloud B2, in the constellation Sagittarius. In 1971 Dr Cyril Ponnamperuma of the NASA Ames Research Centre in California discovered seventeen extraterrestrial amino acids, the so-called 'building blocks of life', in the Murchison meteorite that fell in southern Australia.

Then at the end of 1972, four Australian scientists made a sensational discovery. At a distance of 30,000 light-years from earth, near the centre of our galaxy, they found indications of extra-terrestrial life in a nebula. By means of a computerized radio-telescope in Parkes, New South Wales, investigators found traces of formaldimine, a rare chemical that contributed to the development of animal and plant life on earth.

If such chemical substances already exist in the gaseous clouds that will later condense into planetary systems, then life in the most varied stages of development must be widely disseminated in our stellar system.

All these discoveries show very clearly that life in the universe is not an exception but the rule. So the suggestion that extra-terrestrial intelligences may have visited the earth in the course of its history need not be dismissed out of hand.

Yet people who even hint at such a possibility are either branded as lunatics or attacked venomously. Experienced antagonists generally come up with the argument that the chances of lighting on an advanced civilization within a radius of ten light-years' distance of us are just about nil.

Within this area there are about ten stars, they say, among which really only Alpha Centauri – if that – might conceivably have a planetary system.

Furthermore, it is argued that according to theories of probability the nearest technical civilization might be 300 or even 1,000 light-years distant from us – and how could anyone cover such a distance, seeing that we ourselves are not even capable of getting to the star that is our nearest neighbour, only about 4.3 light-years away!

To argue along these lines is tantamount to saying that our Saturn rocket does not exist, because the head hunters of New Guinea have not yet invented it.

Let us therefore leave out of consideration what might or might not be done by a civilization that is a few hundred years more advanced than ours.

For in all these arguments one important point is overlooked. Since our solar system came into being about five milliard years ago, it has circled round the centre of our galaxy more than twenty times. During this time it has wandered among innumerable stars; and thousands of different stars have been its neighbours in the cosmos.

About a million years ago, for instance, other stars than those we see today were neighbours of our solar system within a radius of ten light-years.

The English scientist, G. V. Foster, has reckoned, in fact, that since the solar system came into being something like 192,000 different stars have come and gone within the radius of ten light-years. And another scientist, Oort, calculated that once in about eleven million light-years a star gets up to three-quarters of a light-year nearer to the sun.

Taking all this into account, the likelihood that at some time in the past a planetary system containing intelligent life came near our sun is very considerable. In such a case it would not have been a matter of very great difficulty for members of a highly-developed extra-terrestrial culture to visit the earth.

The possibility of the existence of extra-terrestrial civilizations millions or even milliards of years ago cannot be excluded. For the age of the Milky Way is reckoned to be not less than thirteen milliard years.

If such extra-terrestrial visitors had left 'visiting cards' in the shape of some kind of artefacts, they would by now have been destroyed by meteorological onslaughts or would have been buried as a result of earth- or rock-movements.

Curiosity is a necessary function of the intellect; so the urge to make one's way into the universe, to discover new worlds, to exchange information, is only natural.

Professor Wheeler of Princeton University, co-inventor of the hydrogen bomb and winner of the Albert Einstein medal, has discovered an absolutely amazing way of bridging the fantastic distances in the cosmos. Wheeler likened the universe to a ring doughnut, on the surface of which all the heavenly bodies are disposed, while in its centre a different universe exists, a sort of super-space. These two worlds lie side by side. In the super-space, however, time and speed have lost their meaning in contrast to our universe.

'In the super-space it makes no sense to ask what will happen next. Words like before, after, subsequent, no longer have any significance. And the word Time no longer means anything,' says Wheeler, one of the few people who really understand the theory of relativity.

If Wheeler's idea is correct, super-space will enable us to travel from one part of the universe to another in a fraction of a second – much faster than light.

Our space-ships will simply plunge into super-space, and come up again at their intended destination in ordinary space, in some other planetary system.

The idea of a kind of super-space has been used by writers of science fiction for years. Naturally, the possible existence of Wheeler's super-space has come under fierce criticism on many sides.

The necessary link in the further development of Einstein's theories about space and time was advanced by the great mathematician Hermann Minkowski (1864–1909) in his famous lecture at the eightieth Natural Sciences Congress in Cologne in 1908. He amalgamated the space-dimension with the time-dimension, into four-dimensional space-time-geometry – the space-time continuum.

Minkowski's space-time can be explained as a kind of hyper- or super-space, in which events do not 'happen', but we simply meet events that already exist. (This would also explain why events could be foreseen or fore-dreamed.) Taking Minkowski's ideas as basis, Einstein reached the inevitable conclusion that the objective physical world is a four-dimensional structure – and that its three space- and one time-dimensions do not mean the same to everyone. '. . . It is much more natural to accept the physical reality of a four-dimensional existence than of one that is three-dimensional . . .' said Einstein. Up to now the speed of light has been regarded in modern physics as the ultimate speed; for no object moving with less than the speed of light can surpass that speed with a finite amount of energy.

But for some time past animated discussions have been going on in the scientific world about the existence of something faster than light, called a tachyon. The debate was initiated by the work of Olexa-Myron Bilaniuk, V. K. Deshpande, E. C. George Sudarshan, and finally Gerald Feinberg.

The question is whether tachyons do exist, and if there is any justification for believing in their existence, in view of the theory of relativity. There certainly is, especially since the Special Theory of Relativity was formulated, because on the assumption that tachyons always, and in every system of inertia, move with a speed greater than that of light, no contradiction arises. A system of inertia is one in which a passive object remains in a state of rest or of uniform motion in a straight line unless constrained. Problems arise only because of our current conception of cause and effect. If the speed of light is exceeded, time runs, so to speak, backwards. Tachyons could, therefore, turn our whole view of the universe upside down.

The scientist, D. J. Thouless, carrying out an imaginary experiment, sends a message to himself at ten o'clock by means of tachyons via the relay-station of a very fast rocket.

But it reaches him at 9.59 – a minute before he despatches it. So he finds out what he is going to do one minute later ...

Stimulated by the possibility that tachyons exist, G. A. Benford, D. L. Book, and W. A. Newcomb have been investigating the idea of telephoning into the past. For, by means of a continuous tachyonic ray, it is (hypothetically) possible to make connection with the past.

If, for example, Richard Wagner had, while he was working on the 'Twilight of the Gods', told his father-in-law Franz Liszt about it over the tachyon-telephone to the past, Liszt might have written a piano version of it before Wagner had actually composed it.

Just because cause and effect are reversed and seem senseless and improbable to us, since we are not normally confronted with such a situation, there is no essential implication that it is an impossibility. At a first glance the idea of taking journeys into the past may seem absurd. But if the tachyon hypothesis should some day be proved to be correct, the possibility of travelling into the past will come nearer.

It would, of course, not be easy to accept the inherent contradictions. If, for instance, someone were to travel back to the year 1938 and shoot Hitler, would the Second World War still break out? The logical answer is: 'Yes.' For, paradoxical as it may seem, although the time-traveller would have shot Hitler, yet as soon as he returned to his own time, the incident would not have occurred – Hitler would not have been shot in *his* own time.

D. H. Schwegler, Professor of Physics at Bremen University, says: '. . . no experiments yet undertaken have shown any proof of the existence of tachyons. In order to make certain of preserving the tachyon-idea at all costs, it might be assumed that no interaction could take place between tachyons and natural matter, and that therefore they could not be verified by experiments undertaken by human beings. Such an assumption would, of course, also do away with the paradoxes of causation. But these tachyons could not be considered as objects for physical research. For all practical purposes they would be non-existent.'

Two different methods have been used to try to bring indirect proof of tachyons travelling at a speed greater than that of light. One such attempt was made by using Cerenkov rays which, as many scientists think, would be given off by tachyons if they were electrically charged. The bluish glow of Cerenkov rays is the optical equivalent of the acoustic bang when the sound barrier is broken.

Nevertheless, the search for tachyons continues. Another way of getting on their track would lie in the possible interaction between tachyons and other elementary particles.

If these tachyons really do exist, one might imagine that intelligent beings separated by enormous distance could carry on interstellar 'telephone conversations' by means of tachyons.

If radio waves at the speed of light were used, two individuals separated by one hundred light-years could be connected telephonically only after two hundred years. By using tachyons, that connection could be made more quickly than can be made now between, say, London and Berlin.

Further, let us assume that there is a highly evolved civilization somewhere in the cosmos. From there a call is made by 'tachyon-telephone' to another such civilization over a distance of several thousand light-years, in order to explain how a particular apparatus should be built: for, by using this apparatus, an astronaut who has been sent to them in the form of a tachyon ray will be rematerialized. . . .

'. . . The Time Traveller came to the place reserved for him without a word. He smiled quietly, in his old way. "Where's my mutton?" he said. "What a treat it is to stick a fork into meat again!"

' "Story!" cried the Editor.

' "Story be damned!" said the Time Traveller. "I want something to eat. I won't say a word until I get some peptones into my arteries. Thanks. And the salt."

' "One word," said I. "Have you been time travelling?"

' "Yes," said the Time Traveller, with his mouth full, nodding his head . . .'

(From: *The Time Machine* by H. G. Wells)

7. An Interstellar Telephone

Strong men are we, and we endure long.
But when – in which of all our lives –
Shall we at last be ready to accept?

R. M. Rilke

Unfortunately tachyons exist only in theory at present, and the probabilities are that it will be a long time before we actually pinpoint them. So, for the moment, we are still a long way from the tachy-telephone.

Meanwhile, a conference at the highest level was held in September 1971 at the astrophysical observatory in Bjurakan, in Soviet Armenia. At this CETI conference (Communication with Extra-Terrestrial Intelligence), the most notable international scientists discussed the possibility of making contact with extra-terrestrial intelligences.

With the words : 'It seems to us to be absolutely essential for members of every nation to take part in the search for extra-terrestrial life', Russian, Hungarian, Czech, American and British delegates were in unaccustomed accord.

The opinions of Western scientists about extra-terrestrial forms of life are accessible to pretty well everyone; but the ideas of experts in the Eastern bloc, which are just as interesting, only seldom reach the general public in the West.

Preparations for the CETI conference by its organizing committee included a series of questions addressed to prominent scientists from all over the world.

Here are the answers given by some top-ranking Soviet delegates :

Question 1: What do you understand by an extra-terrestrial civilization?

L. M. GINDILIS : A complex, highly-organized system, external to this world, capable of independent action and abstract thought.

F. A. TSITSIN : A group of individuals interested in one-another and in similar social forms.

V. G. KURT : A community, capable of discrimination, possessing technical skills and installations (for the control of traffic, storage, and the transmission of information).

I. S. SHKLOVSKI : Similar to earthly civilization, but not necessarily anthropomorphic; and probably at an entirely different stage of technical and scientific development.

S. A. KAPLAN : At any material level, capable of disseminating reasonable information beyond its own solar system.

I. A. NOVIKOFF : A complex organism (a 'machine' in the cybernetic sense), that is actively conscious of its environment and capable of abstract thought.

Question 2: Does any other civilization exist apart from the one on earth?

E. A. DIBAY : Our civilization is not unique; I assume that there are others.

W. L. GINZBURG : I have no reason to doubt the existence of other civilizations. But we might find that ours is the only one in the Milky Way.

L. M. GINDILIS : This is simply a matter of guesswork, though it appears to me to be quite probable. I hardly think that our civilization is unique, but I would believe that it is a rare phenomenon.

N. S. KARDASHEV : I believe that there are a great many civilizations in the universe.

S. B. PIKEL'NER : In my opinion, ours is not the only civilization in our galaxy, if only because certain fundamental organic components have been found in interstellar dust-clouds.

I. S. SHKLOVSKI : I would say it is possible that ours is the only civilization in the universe within our sphere of observation.

Question 3: Do you believe that contact with an extra-

terrestrial civilization is possible?

S. A. KAPLAN: I believe it to be absolutely possible. I see no physical, technical, nor semantic problems.

V. A. AMBARZUMJAN: I can see no reason why such contact should not take place.

N. S. KARDASHEV: There need be no trouble about making contact. To begin with, one might consider using electro-magnetic waves.

N. T. PETROVICH: I believe that there is every chance of making contact, for the laws of physics are the same all over the universe, and so too are the origins of life.

I. S. SHKLOVSKI: I certainly believe that it will be possible to make contact; but I expect it to be much more complicated than people think.

V. S. TROITSKI: Making contact should be feasible, probably by using electro-magnetic waves.

Question 4: Is it possible, in principle, for us to understand messages received by extra-terrestrial signals?

V. A. AMBARZUMJAN: It should be possible in principle to convey mathematical and logical interrelations between objects; but difficulties might arise over interpretation.

E. A. DIBAY: If you refer to history, you will find that science has always found a way to break any code.

B. N. PANOVKIN: In principle it is impossible to extract information contained in signals emitted on unfamiliar systems.

S. B. PIKEL'NER: No doubt the interpretation of signals is highly complicated; but in principle it must be possible to find a way of doing it.

Question 5: What methods will be used in searching for extra-terrestrial signals? Will ordinary astronomic and radio-astronomic investigation suffice?

V. A. AMBARZUMJAN: Until we know what kind of signals are being used, there is no point in searching. If any practical ideas are put forward a search could and should be attempted. An extension of radio-astronomic observation of signals of natural origin might conceivably lead to the discovery of artificial signals.

V. L. GINZBURG: An international undertaking established on a broad basis should organize the installation of an enormous special radio-telescope. Even if the search for signals should turn out to be fruitless, such an instrument would still be useful to astronomical science.

N. T. PETROVICH: Some extension of radio-astronomical equipment that would function uninterruptedly over a long period should, one might suppose, be capable of carrying out a programme of this description . . .

S. B. PIKEL'NER: The likelihood of discovering such signals is slight.

V. S. TROITSKI: Ordinary radio-astronomical processes, methods and equipment would not be adequate for the purpose. Special equipment as well as a definite programme would have to be arranged.

Question 6: In which direction should search be made for extra-terrestrial signals?

N. S. KARDASHEV: The optimum wave-range for signals must be determined. A continuous and unbroken watch must be kept for signals in the millimetre, centimetre, and decimetre-wave-lengths, together with a study of radio- and X-ray-emanations from 100 stars similar to our sun.

N. T. PETROVICH: Contact between two interstellar civilizations might be simulated by means of two computers, in order to ascertain from them what kind of signals appear suitable . . .

A. D. SAKHAROV: We must extend both our installations and our knowledge; quite probably we may not yet have reached the standard of knowledge of radiation which other civilizations expect. We must increase the sensitivity of our instruments and improve our methods.

V. S. TROITSKI: If we are proposing to look for signals, we shall have to investigate radiations from the nearest stars up to a distance of 1,000 light-years. In considering the main problem, account must be taken of the length of life of a technically advanced civilization.

I. S. SHKLOVSKI: Serious theoretical analysis of the problem, of its philosophical, biological, temporal and futuristic aspects, is urgently necessary. In addition, we shall have to develop special apparatuses and a programme for carrying out observations. And then there will be the further difficulty of decoding the signals.

Question 7: What are the probable consequences of making contact?

V. L. GINZBURG: I cannot take seriously the idea of possibly detrimental influences. Other results would depend on distance – that is to say, on the length of time signals took to reach us.

V. A. AMBARZUMJAN: Although it might not begin with a shock, such contact would in the distant future have a tremendous influence upon human society. . . .

The search for extra-terrestrial signals did in fact begin in America in 1960 with Project Ozma, which was initiated by Professor F. Drake under the overall direction of the prominent Russian-American astronomer Otto Struve (1897–1967).

In the early morning hours of 8th April 1960, Drake began the search for signals of extra-terrestrial origin. The radio-telescope at the Green Bank Observatory in West Virginia, USA, was aimed by him and his colleagues at the stars Tau Ceti and Epsilon Eridani in turn. They hoped to intercept signals on the 21-centimetre wave-length. This particular wave-length is the natural frequency radiated by hydrogen atoms and, so Drake believed, would therefore probably be used for transmissions by an advanced civilization.

Before beginning the undertaking, Drake had reckoned that the only signals that could possibly be intercepted would be those sent from one of the planets of either of the two stars (each more than eleven light-years distant) by means of a 200-metre mirror over a one-million-watt transmitter. The chances of success were, therefore, from the outset seen to be practically non-existent, for the Green Bank radio-telescope is not sensitive enough for such an undertaking. After 150 hours of strenuous, uninterrupted listening, the project was temporarily called off.

Drake argues that the development of technological facilities on earth has hitherto been carried on for only a very short time.

Further, that a civilization needs about a hundred years to advance from complete ignorance about electro-magnetic communication to perfect mastery.

Of course, a century is quite a long time in relation to human life; but in the cosmic time-scale it is very short, in fact only 10^8 of the life of a stellar system. Since it is only the lapse of cosmic time that counts, a planet would – in comparison with that – be achieving absolute command of technology from a state of absolute ignorance at a single bound.

Once a civilization has reached this state of scientific knowledge, it can begin to initiate contact with similar civilizations over interstellar distances. The earth has now reached this stage. In view of the constant birth of new stars, civilizations at a technological level similar to our own may also be expected to ensue.

It may be assumed without further discussion that most civilizations in the cosmos are more advanced than ours. But, of course, the use of technology on a planet might for one reason or another stop – either because of self-destruction or as a result of some cosmic catastrophe; or possibly owing to a change in the philosophy of a form of life that does without technology.

The number of civilizations using radio-waves in any stellar system is obviously connected with the number of newly-evolving civilizations appearing annually. To these must be added the average length of life of civilizations that have already reached the stage of using an electro-magnetic system of communication.

1. Aura of the leaf of a celandine, photographed by Semyon and Valentina Kirlian

2. Unusual picture of a cell meiosis. Photograph by Dr R. Dietz, Max-Planck Institute of Cell Biology ▽

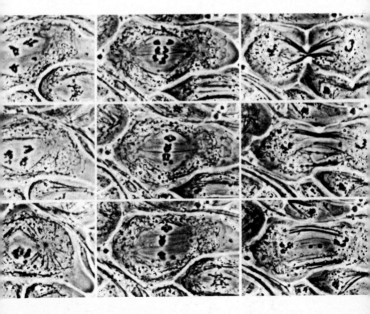

◁
3. The Count de Saint-Germain

4. On 29 October 1971, L. G.
Lawrence received extra-
terrestrial biological signals
by means of this apparatus ▽

◁

5. Boundary stone from Mesopotamia, eleventh century B.C. The moon, as basis of the Babylonian calendar, is shown between Venus and the sun

6. Six UFOs in formation, seen against a starry sky; photographed from a N.A.S.A. orbit-tracking station ▽

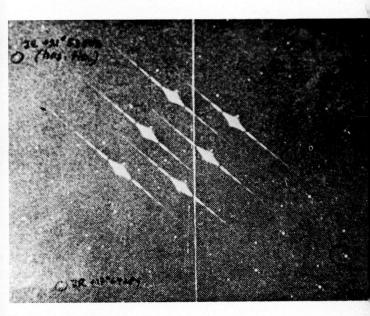

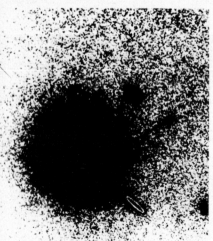

△
7. Fresco, 1335-50, in the
Dečani Monastery, Jugoslavia.
An angel on a journey ?

8. A Quasar ◁

Where an intelligent civilization has had no more than a brief spell of life, contact will be possible comparatively infrequently. In our own case, it looks very much as if we should cut short any chance of survival by self-destruction.

'The number of civilizations in the cosmos that might be reached does not', in Professor Drake's opinion, 'depend upon the number of planets that exist, but on a m' h more serious question: is there intelligent life on earth? Let us be optimistic and assume that there is,' he says, 'for in that case there will also be intelligent life in the cosmos.'

Meanwhile our technology has progressed so far that we can send and receive signals up to a distance of a hundred light-years. If we add the possibilities of space-stations or installations on the moon, the radius might be increased to several thousand light-years.

This would be useful only in searching for signals that could be intercepted; any hope of communication between ourselves and others would, purely on account of the time-question, be illusory, for the process might take thousands of years.

As we mentioned earlier, the most satisfactory frequency for the undertaking would be the 21-centimetre wave-length, and success would be most likely to be achieved in this range.

Low frequencies within 500 MHz (60-centimetre wave-length) would be jammed by the natural radiations of the Milky Way; and high frequencies over 6,000 MHz (5-centimetre wave-length) are vulnerable to atmospheric disturbances from the earth. Bernard Oliver, an electrical engineer, made attempts to solve the problem of the possibility of receiving 'cosmic information' by working on the basis of Professor Drake's theories. He compiled a code of call-signs that might conceivably convey information to some other, far-away, civilization. This information would be transmitted on the 21-centimetre wave-length in a series of irregular impulses.

A pictorial transmission would, to begin with, produce an apparently meaningless pattern of 1,271 black dots and white spaces. But the number 1,271 is the product of the two prime numbers 31×41. There are, therefore, two possible ways of arranging the dots and spaces in rectangular form: either by dividing the figure into 31 lines with 41 dots and 41 spaces; or into 41 lines with 31 dots and 31 spaces. The former of these alternatives produces a highly ingenious design or picture.

Obviously, a civilization would wish in the first instance to project some description of its physical appearance. So we humans would show up as creatures with two arms and two legs, male and female and children. If the above design is suitably arranged, figures can be represented to show man, woman, child, sun, and planets – which of the sun's planets is inhabited, and much else.

Since the development of this idea, the Russians have programmed computers to decipher these so-called binary codes immediately they are received. Thus, by using mathematical symbols, equations, television pictures, or the binary code, a language applicable to interstellar communication might be evolved.

The Dutch Professor H. Freudenthal, of Utrecht University, Holland, invented a special language that he called 'Lincos' (*lingua cosmica*), based on the logistic language of the two philosophers, Bertrand Russell and Alfred Whitehead, in order to make it understandable to intelligent beings, even if they had nothing in common with us apart from intelligence. Freudenthal was inclined to suggest that a language of this description might conceivably exist already for cosmic interchange of ideas.

Although we have not as yet intercepted any extraterrestrial message, it is none the less possible that interstellar conversations may be passing back and forth continually within our galaxy.

Professor Carl Sagan, the well-known exobiologist (that is, one who investigates extra-terrestrial life), says on this point: 'We may well be comparable with inhabitants of an isolated valley in New Guinea, who communicate with neighbouring villages by means of drums and runners without knowing that there is an extensive international radio system all around, passing over and under and through them.'

In addition to contact signals, we might also be able to tap radio and television programmes broadcast by extraterrestrial civilizations.

Robert Jungk, the 'futurologist', says: 'One might wonder whether there are not more urgent matters to consider here on earth, such as the perils arising from social injustices and the neglect of forward planning.'

To this the advocates of making contact reply: 'The fact that we are faced by such exceptionally serious difficulties, and that we have hitherto failed to deal with them, is the very reason for taking long odds on the chance of getting advice from the cosmos.'

The first steps towards making contact have already been taken, with some prospects of success.

Since the setting up at Cornell University of the great radio-telescope, with its diameter of 300 metres, signals can be intercepted from distances that have until recently been looked upon as 'astronomical'.,

This 'hearing aid' into the universe was installed near Arecibo in the mountains of Puerto Rico. Professor Drake's protracted studies in this field were rewarded by his appointment as Director of the establishment. Another and even more sensitive apparatus is being set up in the State of New Mexico, USA, to the west of Soccoro. It is planned in this case to use twenty-seven smaller radio-telescopes, to form a mobile, interchangeable system, which will, it is hoped, make possible the interception of even the faintest signals from the uttermost limits of any part of the universe perceptible to us with hitherto unattainable distinctness. In this case, a VLA radio-telescope will be used. (VLA=*V*ery *L*arge *A*rray).

New methods of communication brought about the discovery of the optical LASER (Light Amplification of Stimulated Energy Radiation) and MASER (Microwave Amplification of Stimulated Energy Radiation).

If several million Joule (electrical units of work named after James Prescott Joule, 1818–1889) were radiated by means of a 200-metre reflector at intervals of seconds on the 21-centimetre wave-length, such signals would be capable of travelling distances of up to 1,000 light-years.

All technical methods at our disposal at the present time for making contact with extra-terrestrial intelligences are conditioned by the time-barrier. For, as we said above, mutual exchange of information might in some cases take hundreds or even thousands of years. Hence, telepathy should be considered as a means of interstellar communication. This would do away with all the drawbacks of electromagnetic methods of communication – the enormous cost, technical inadequacy, and, above all, the time-factor. For telepathic communication takes place practically without loss of time, at the speed of thought, in the twinkling of an eye – instantaneously.

At the International Astronautical Congress held in Paris in 1963, someone suggested telepathy as the quickest, most satisfactory and cheapest means of communication – only to be ridiculed by most of the delegates. But some of these began to think again when it became known that even at that time eight Soviet teams of investigators (and by now there are many more) were studying the transmission of thought from a physiological aspect.

In the 1930s, not long before his death, Konstantin E. Ziolkowski (1857–1935), the father of Russian astronautics, had expressed himself as convinced of the necessity for the use of telepathy in future space-flight. Ziolkowski regarded telepathy as one of the greatest essentials for the further development of humanity. And in his opinion, man would solve the problems of the human spirit by penetrating the mysteries of psychical phenomena, while space-travel would open up the universe to him.

As early as 1890, Ziolkowski put his views on the subject of aeronautics on to paper. In 1898 he was the first to advocate the use of liquid fuel for rockets – oxygen and hydrogen. And in 1903 he published his views on the movement of rockets. He showed that rockets can function even in a vacuum. At the same time he produced the first speculations about the possibilities of interplanetary travel, and of how a satellite might be put into orbit. Ziolkowski believed that humanity would reach its highest fulfilment through knowledge of space-travel and parapsychology.

Nowadays the Soviet Union spends more than any other State on the study of parapsychology – the annual budget is almost unlimited: it is estimated to be something over £10,000,000; and more than twenty research centres have been set up for it.

In the Eastern bloc, parapsychology has been developed into an important department of the natural sciences, in close connection with physiology, biology, and bionomics. In the West, on the other hand, the subject is still treated as the illegitimate child of psychology. Up to 1930, it is true, some very promising experiments were carried out in ESP (extra-sensory perception); but these had to be broken off, largely for financial reasons.

A series of systematic experiments was carried out in 1927 at Duke University, Durham, USA, under the auspices of Professor J. B. Rhine. In these experiments it was shown quite unequivocally that extra-sensory perceptions such as telepathy, clairvoyance, and prophecy really exist, and that these faculties are latent in almost everyone.

Rhine's 'guinea-pigs' for the experiments were chosen at random. The tests were conducted with cards marked with various symbols:

(1) The subject of the experiment must discover by means of thought transference which symbols the experimenter was thinking of.
(2) The subject must tell by clairvoyance which cards (unknown to himself as well as to the experimenter) were covered.
(3) He must prophesy the order in which cards would be ejected by an automatic mixing machine.

The experiments were evaluated statistically, with the

following results:

When twenty-five cards are used, with five different symbols, the average chance according to the law of probabilities is five.

For 200 attempts (eight packs) requiring $6\frac{1}{2}$ correct answers, the odds are 1 : 150.

No odds are quoted for an unbroken series of correct answers, even when only small numbers of attempts are made.

But the odds are 1 : 2 million for nine correct answers in a row; and for giving fifteen correct answers in a row, the odds are 1 : 30 milliards.

The results actually obtained excluded any possibility of chance.

During the 1940s the English mathematician S. G. Soal conducted tens of thousands of carefully supervised tests with these cards, and produced some remarkable results. His two 'subjects' were both well above the average in the number of correct answers they gave. Interestingly enough, all these experiments showed that it is hard to distinguish clairvoyance from telepathy.

In 1937 a telepathic experiment was carried out quite unexpectedly between Sir Hubert Wilkins, the polar airman, and Harold Sherman, the well-known author. Radio contact had been lost with the polar flier S. Levanewsky, and he had been reported missing. Wilkins had offered to carry out a search, and Sherman proposed to keep in touch with him by telepathy during the operation. Sherman had spent many years in cultivating his supersensory powers. The two men arranged that they would concentrate on one another three times a week at a given time, and that they would make notes of the results. Wilkins kept a diary and Sherman sent the record of his telepathic interception to the American psychologist Professor Gardener Murphy in New York, each time on the day following that on which the agreed contact had been made.

Wilkins started his search from Point Barrow and Aklavik

on the Mackenzie River. From there he covered something over 3,000 kilometres of the polar regions in his aircraft. Sherman kept to the agreed schedule of contacts, but Wilkins was not always able to do so. None the less, Sherman 'saw' Wilkins in the most various situations. On one occasion, for instance, he thought Wilkins would be on the way to his destination, but 'discovered' him in a dance hall. It turned out later that Wilkins had been obliged to return to Canada on account of bad weather, and that he had received and accepted an invitation to a dance in Regina.

Another time, Sherman 'observed' Wilkins chopping a hole in the polar ice to catch fish. Again, he was 'present' when a fire in an Eskimo house proved impossible to extinguish because the water was frozen. In the same way, Sherman 'perceived' that the undertaking was unexpectedly called off, and that Wilkins was on the way home much sooner than had been expected.

The *New York Times* had intended to keep in constant touch by radio while the expedition was in progress; but owing to poor weather conditions radio connection was made only thirteen times during the five months, against sixty-eight good telepathic contacts.

The telepathic faculties of primitive peoples are sufficiently well known, but still remain an unfathomable mystery to men living in a world adjusted to technique. Telepathy as a means of communication is a very much quicker form of 'wireless' than anything the technical world can show with its telephones, teleprinters, and radio sets. It is an intellectual capacity that puts all our technical resources in the shade.

'W. R. Benzies, an ex-Colonial Officer in Matabele Land, Southern Rhodesia, tells the following story,' said Willy Schrödter in his book *Neuer Ausflug ins Wundersame* (A New Excursion into Mystery): 'One day I received a telegram about a Zulu rising. It had been two days on the way. I showed the wire to my native sergeant, intending to ask him to issue warnings. But he told me that this would not be necessary, because – *as everyone knew* – the Zulus had already been driven back the day before.

'Official confirmation of the incident, which had occurred thousands of miles away, did not arrive until some days later.'

Many indications show that in olden times man possessed strongly marked ESP faculties that have gradually been lost with an increasingly technological environment. But every now and then these faculties crop up again in individual cases as a kind of atavistic talent.

In the animal world supersensory perceptions are an important factor for the chance of survival. How else can one explain the circumstance that, days before a bush fire breaks out, animals will flee from the district where it is going to happen?

Many of the inhabitants of Freiburg actually owe their lives to the instinct of a bird.

At about half past seven in the evening of 27th November 1944 people in the neighbourhood of the City Park noticed the nervous, excited quacking of a drake in that park. This drake was reputed to have forebodings when something unusual was going to happen. At any rate, those who knew the bird and heard its agitated voice went down into their air-raid shelters, just in case. No warning siren was sounded, but at eight o'clock, the centre of Freiburg was within twenty minutes reduced to a pile of rubble in an air raid. There were many casualties, including the bird whose instinct had saved the lives of others.

On 27th November 1953, the ninth anniversary of the event, the city of Freiburg unveiled a memorial to its good genius, the drake.

Year after year flocks of migrant birds travel over the same route for hundreds or thousands of miles in order to return to the nests they left months before. But if that place has been disturbed by some catastrophe, they seem to know about it, for they do not go back there.

And when elephants feel that death is near, they will for weeks wander along paths they have never trodden before, until they find their 'graveyard' – a place they have never seen before.

Experiments with termites have shown that they obey the behests of their queen, even if they are shut off from her by a leaden screen.

One could go on indefinitely giving examples of supersensory perception by animals. But that is a subject on its own, so let us return to consideration of the telepathic faculties of man.

Some remarkable and unexpectedly successful ESP experiments were carried out in 1966 by the Russians in what was known as the 'Moscow-Siberia telepathy test'. Karl Nikolajew, a journalist, was invited to prove to a delegation of members of the Soviet Academy of Sciences the truth of his claim that telepathy was effective over great distances. The meeting was held in a completely isolated room and, under the sceptical eyes of the experts, Nikolajew was required to identify objects described to him telepathically by Juri Kamenski, a biophysicist, 3,000 kilometres away in Moscow. Kamenski took a variety of things out of sealed packets, one after another. Nikolajew described them in the greatest detail according to Kamenski's emanations. In one case, for example, Kamenski concentrated on a screwdriver with a black plastic handle. Nikolajew's description was: long – thin – artificial material – black. The same thing happened with a spiral spring. Nikolajew's reply: round – metallic – shiny – a sort of coil.

The Russians have recognized how important telepathy is, and have included it as a subject in their training programme for cosmonauts.

In America, Edgar D. Mitchell, the Apollo XIV astronaut, carried out an ESP test with an experimental group on earth. But no details of this have yet been published.

Up to the present no one has succeeded in explaining how telepathy works. All that is known is that it does work. But a likely theory would seem to be that telepathic radiations are a hitherto unrecognized source of energy; and also that telepathic faculties can be cultivated by training.

In view of the immense perspectives opened to us by telepathy, serious consideration should be given to organizing a study centre for research into fresh possibilities of making interstellar contact and especially by psychic means.

It may be taken as certain that extra-terrestrial civilizations exist in which telepathy and other ESP faculties have been developed to a high degree of perfection.

How can we tell that telepathic messages are not reaching us constantly without our recognizing them? Humanity may in former times have been less insensitive, more ready to accept, and possibly in actual telepathic communication with extra-terrestrial intelligences. Might it be that our prayers are an unconscious relic of those days?

Among primitive peoples it still sometimes happens that the medicine man goes into a trance in order to ask his god for guidance. And may it not be that the occasional genius who appears in the course of the centuries is influenced by one of the more advanced intelligences in the universe?

In addition to telepathy, there is also the phenomenon of ESP, to which increasing significance is being attached. Both Professor Hornell Hart, of Duke University, and Charles Tarte, Professor of Psychology at the University of California, devote a great deal of time to this subject. It is also known in America as OOBES (Out Of The Body Experiences).

References to such experiences are found throughout the history of mankind. In particular, they form an essential part of yoga training. But what, in actual fact, is meant by astral projection? It is said that in this condition the spirit can detach itself from the body and that the 'double' can travel to every imaginable place. Against this dualism scientists reason that mind and spirit are two aspects of the same thing; and that, although an organism possesses both, they can never be separated. On the other hand, advocates of ESP projection counter with the argument that the brain is simply a kind of 'transformer' for the spirit, and that therefore the spirit can quite well project itself out of the body.

A rather less dynamic, though typical description of the phenomenon is, more or less, the following: I am lying in bed: I feel that I am detached from my body. I feel as though I were floating above myself. I have an unaccustomed view of my face and am fully conscious of my surroundings. I feel indescribably free. But it is very difficult to sustain this condition for any length of time; after a while I know I must return to my body.

A much more dramatic account is taken from the Memoirs of F. Wallner, and has been attested by General von Gerlach.

The Evangelical Archbishop of Uppsala once visited Berlin on his way through Prussia and was invited to dinner by King Frederick William IV.

In the course of the evening, conversation turned to the still wide-spread superstitions and uncanny faculties hereditary in many families in Lapland. The Archbishop said that his Government had once commissioned him to go there, accompanied by a doctor and a civil servant, for the express purpose of getting to the bottom of these stories. Not even the Archbishop's companions were told the real purpose of the expedition.

Having arrived at their destination, they all became the guests of a well-to-do Laplander who, as it happened, had the reputation of being a magician. He was a pleasant, hospitable man named Peter Lärdal, said the Archbishop.

On the morning of the third day of their visit, the Archbishop asked quite casually at breakfast whether his host minded being decried as a sorcerer. The Laplander replied with a broad smile that His Lordship need feel no embarrassment, because he, Lärdal, knew that the real purpose of this visit was to investigate superstition in Lapland and to eradicate it if possible, by calling to account those mainly responsible.

In his surprise, the Archbishop made no bones about

acknowledging that it was so, and added that this kind of 'nonsense' could be reconciled neither with the Christian religion nor with scientific knowledge.

To this, Peter Lärdal replied that he could not prevent His Lordship from doing whatever he considered to be his duty; but that the whole business had nothing to do with 'nonsense', and that he was ready to prove it immediately. He would separate his soul from his body, and the Archbishop should tell him where to send it. When he returned he would give proof that he had actually been to that place.

Torn between curiosity and his principles, the Archbishop finally agreed, privately hoping to come on the track of some fraud. He suggested, therefore, that Lärdal's spirit should go to Uppsala and bring back news of his wife.

Meanwhile Lärdal had fetched a pan containing some dried herbs to which he set fire. He said that he would inhale the fumes of the herbs, which would make him lose consciousness. In no circumstances must he be touched, because that would kill him. He would regain consciousness after about an hour.

So Lärdal lay in his chair for an hour like a dead man, his face deathly pale. Then he woke up twitching convulsively and described the Archbishop's kitchen in Uppsala. In order to prove that he had been there, he said, he had taken the Lady's wedding ring and had hidden it in the bottom of the coal scuttle; she had taken it off because she was cooking.

The Archbishop wrote to his wife at once and asked her to tell him what she had been doing that morning, and where she had been. The answer arrived a fortnight later. She said she would never forget that morning because she had been making a cake and had therefore taken off her wedding ring and laid it on the table. The ring had disappeared. For a few moments a well-dressed Laplander had been in the kitchen. He had made no reply when she asked his business, and had left without saying anything. This man, she supposed, must have taken the ring.

Later the ring was in fact found at the bottom of the coal scuttle.

Between 1965 and 1971 laboratory experiments were carried out with Robert A. Monroe, an American, under the scientific control of Professor Charles T. Tarte. These showed that astral projection is a reality. Monroe undertook travels in his astral body and on his return described in detail strange places and conversations that were confirmed after investigation.

Another interesting experiment was carried out in England in 1969. Four people, under the auspices of a hypnotist, agreed that they would attempt to project themselves on to another planet under hypnosis. A fifth man offered himself as observer.

The hypnotist put himself and the four people into a deep sleep. The experiment lasted for about two hours. As soon as they awoke, they all, without exchanging a word with each other, immediately wrote an account of their experience. They were all in agreement in their description of a voyage through space, of a strange planet with curious, leafless trees whose branches curled round in tight rings, of lakes of oil, a great red sun, fissured red rocks, and vast expanses of desert . . . The timing of the experiment was verified by the observer, as well as the fact that the hypnotist had put himself and the others into their trance and had then kept silence.

Can anyone gauge the immense possibilities that would follow if the spirit should really succeed in projecting itself through time and space to other places – even to the stars?

In this connection, a highly controversial experiment leaps to the mind, even though it probably never happened . . .

8. The Impossible Experiment

When it comes to it – what are man's truths?
They are his irrefutable errors.

F. Nietzsche

Rumours about what is said to have taken place in 1943 will probably never come to an end; nor is it likely that the whole truth about the 'Philadelphia Experiment' will ever be brought to light any more than will the man-o'-war that vanished with all its crew on that never-to-be-forgotten day. Nothing, apart from hints and vague theories, has ever come out to explain what really happened. Rumour, of course, has never died down, whether whispered by a high Government official, by a famous scientist, or by the man in the street. But does not a grain of truth lurk in every piece of gossip? Probably even in what one hears about something that is impossible – such as the Philadelphia Experiment. Nothing much has ever been written on this particular saga; Alan Lambert is one of the few to have made a detailed study of it.

This is what is said to have happened. It chanced that nobody was standing at the bar of the sailors' pub near the harbour at Philadelphia. Next moment, three naval ratings in full uniform were standing there, as though conjured up out of the blue. The barmaid had just loaded her tray with glasses and bottles for customers waiting at the tables. She shrieked with fright and dropped the tray. Civilians and sailors sitting around watched in stunned silence. The trio vanished from the scene as quickly as it had appeared.

'I'm getting the creeps,' said one of the customers.

'I've got cold shivers down my back,' muttered another. And a third seemed no longer to be enjoying his drink; he stared incredulously and shook himself.

At Norfolk, Virginia, sailors, civilians and officials standing on the pier at the naval base, saw the tender of a small destroyer appear from the void, only to disappear again.

The witnesses were thunderstruck.

Almost a thousand miles away from Norfolk, the tender of a destroyer lay at anchor beside a pier at the naval base of Philadelphia; it vanished for a few minutes, then reappeared.

All this happened in November 1943, in broad daylight, and it remains as one of the great unsolved mysteries of the Second World War. Naval Intelligence refuses to give any information; and no documents or log books, normally available to qualified investigators, are open for inspection. According to official statements, no such data exist.

There may be a connection between this secret and the death of a man who stumbled upon a series of events said to have a bearing on an immensely important scientific discovery. Apart from a few Government officials, believed to have been sworn to silence, nobody knows anything further about it. The story begins in the early part of 1942, when a civilian whose identity has never been disclosed, visited the headquarters of the Naval Intelligence Department in Washington DC. The US Navy had been approaching various independent American scientists with the request that they should put forward new ideas about unorthodox weapons and methods of warfare. America was at the time in what was perhaps one of the darkest periods in the whole of her history. The Japanese were in control of the Pacific and, since the fearful attack on Pearl Harbour, the US Navy no longer existed. President Roosevelt raged furiously. This affair, he said, would go down in history as 'a day of infamy'.

As a result of Pearl Harbour, it was necessary to rebuild the American fleet, and to mobilize men and munitions of war on an enormous scale before facing the enemy. Military strategy had also to be replanned. All this was to take two years. Many of the naval vessels dated not only from the First World War but from even earlier times and were completely obsolete, as also were plans of attack and systems of camouflage. The US Naval Intelligence was, therefore, in urgent need of expert advice, particularly on the subject of camouflage.

At this time, a scientist – unnamed, but understood to be well known – visited the Office of Naval Research (ONR). 'Give me a ship, gentlemen,' he said, 'and I will show you an impossibility – the perfect camouflage.' Asked about the kind of camouflage he envisaged, the caller explained precisely what he proposed doing. The officers could not believe their ears as the scientist said quite calmly and dispassionately that he could make a ship – any ship – disappear. As this man was one of the most distinguished of American physicists, whose credibility was obviously indisputable, his statement was taken seriously.

Later on, this obscure affair was still further complicated by the death and the anomalous life of a highly qualified astrophysicist Dr Morris K. Jessup, whose name has always been connected with this mysterious case. Dr Jessup revealed the background of a secret experiment which caused a ship and its crew to vanish. It was an experiment that spelt doom for an unknown number of sailors who took part in it.

In the same way as at Peenemünde in Germany, research programmes involving a number of unorthodox experiments were carried out in the USA during the Second World War. Their aim in both cases was to bring the war to an end as quickly as possible by using new and uncompromising methods. Dr Jessup took part in a number of these secret projects. As a physicist himself, he knew of Albert Einstein's visit to Roosevelt, when Einstein had proposed to take things to their logical conclusion and develop a super-bomb. Actually, his suggestion is believed also to have been concerned with yet another issue, to do with certain electrical and magnetic fields of force that – almost incredibly – could make men and things invisible. What side-effects would be caused was not known. No information has been given about Dr Jessup's part in these experiments.

A list of the names of the scientists concerned in this

top-secret programme is said to be kept in the special files of the US Navy Office and to be, to all intents and purposes, inaccessible, except to the highest ranking personnel and upon direct authorization by the Pentagon. At the end of the Second World War, Dr Jessup was appointed as astronomer to Drake University, and later transferred to the University of Michigan. Among other things, during the early post-war years, he investigated UFOs, which were regarded as a particularly acute problem at the time, and he discussed them in several of his books. At the beginning of the 1950s, Professor Jessup received a number of letters that appeared at a first glance to be the ramblings of a crank. They touched on the origins of UFOs, but also dealt with a number of things that had happened during the war and that were known to Dr Jessup; he had himself co-operated in some of them.

The writer of the letters connected the source of the energy that powered UFOs directly with the wartime research project for the development of a perfect camouflage for naval vessels.

Professor Jessup published these letters in one of his books; and although they sounded eccentric, to say the least, the Naval Secret Service and the Office of Naval Research displayed an immediate interest in them. Attention was focused particularly on the letters referring to the 1943 experiment, which gave reasons for its failure. The writer, it was clear, had a remarkable knowledge of physics. The letters bore the signature Carlos Miguel Allende, and were despatched from New Kensington, Pennsylvania, Post Office Box 223, State Delivery Area No. 1. Some later letters were signed Carl M. Allen.

Dr Jessup was interested in these letters particularly because Allende alleged that he was familiar with the naval experiment based on Einstein's electrical field theory; it had been imperfectly carried out, he said. He added that, on the basis of the theory, it was possible to travel through enormous distances in space without the passage of time. Surprising to Jessup, as well as to the US Office of Naval Research, were Allende's mathematical formulae which are believed to have amended certain scientific data that had until then been accepted as factual. A check by computer of Allende's results is said to have shown them to be correct. Furthermore, Allende made reference to a Dr Franklin Reno, who is thought to have been connected with some unsuccessful experiments during the war. Intelligence Services are understood to have been particularly shocked by Allende's comment: 'The Navy was afraid of the consequences.' The 'consequences' referred to concerned the complete invisibility of ships at sea. In that particular experiment, a ship is said to have been surrounded by a magnetic field of something like 90-metres radius. 'Within this compass, each man only saw the others on the ship as phantoms walking in a void. Outside it, on the circumference of this field of force, an observer would see nothing except the shape of the ship's hull outlined in the water.' The facts in Allende's description were known only to a few of the highest civil and military authorities in the US Government. Statements made later by some of Dr Jessup's close friends showed that Allende's intelligence was not new to him.

After the publication of Allende's letters by Dr Jessup, the Pentagon took action. Admiral Ransom Bennett, Chief of the Office of Naval Research, was handed a packet by one of his assistants, containing a copy of Jessup's book, together with notes made by three people, discussing the contents. When the Admiral asked what it was all about and was told: 'the Philadelphia Experiment', he dismissed the young man immediately, and dialled a private number. A secret conference on the highest level was called at once; and two hours later a meeting took place of people from the Pentagon and the armed forces, of leading scientists and senior officials of the CIA and FBI.

On the same day, a detachment of FBI agents flew to New Kensington in Pennsylvania to look for Carlos Miguel Allende. He had disappeared.

Inhabitants of the village remembered him as a little, dark man called Allen, and referred the visitors to an elderly married couple named Carter, who had lived on the outskirts of the place for forty years, and with whom Allen had lodged. The Federal Agents soon discovered that not only Allende but also the Carters had vanished. Enquiries at the local police station showed that the Carters were 'nice people', but that they seldom came to the village except to do their weekly shopping. They had never had any contact even with their nearest neighbours, and though resident for forty years had no friends – a fact that surprised the head of the police when he thought about it. When asked what they looked like, all that the neighbours could say was that they were an elderly couple, with dark skins, just like Allende. 'Queer people', was the general opinion; but no details emerged. No satisfactory information was given, and the recurrent answer: 'I don't really know; they were queer, not like us', did not reveal anything useful.

The FBI agents did not even know the reason why they had been sent to look for Allende, and finally dropped the enquiry as useless. Apart from J. Edgar Hoover, then head of the FBI, and two of his closest assistants, nobody is thought to have been informed of the background to the affair. The problem was concerned not only with national security, but was immensely important from the scientific angle. Allende knew about an experiment that one would rather have had forgotten. It was obviously urgent that he should at all costs be found.

Why is all information about the Philadelphia Experiment held back to this day? Why do top scientists and secret service men waste time over the letters of a 'lunatic'? Why are the Secret Service and the counter-espionage so much interested?

The Allende-Jessup correspondence leads one to the inevitable conclusion that the US Navy carried out an experiment during the Second World War whereby a ship was, with partial success, made invisible. The story can be more or less reconstructed from fragmentary reports. According to these, scientists succeeded in altering the molecular structure of matter, thereby causing a ship to vanish with all on board. It reappeared, then disappeared again, and the process was repeated several times. Nobody understood what was happening. It was hoped that the ship would return to normal when the field of energy had exhausted itself. But a further and unexpected development was that the ship was found to have transferred from one place to another at, literally, lightning speed. It did not simply flicker, like a light being switched on and off; it reappeared elsewhere. And no one knows in how many different places it turned up while it lay at anchor in Philadelphia.

The most terrible fate befell the crew, as Allende wrote. The men walked in a void and, after a few steps, vanished suddenly in a burst of flame. Allende had no doubt but that the experiment was a complete failure since the ship was not even manoeuvrable. He had, he said, been in Philadelphia himself at the time. All in all, he continued, the thing had aroused such horror among all who knew of it that the whole project was abandoned as impossible, impracticable, and hideously dangerous.

As Allende described it, the men had turned into blazing fiery torches, had lost their reason, had taken a few steps, and had then simply disappeared into the void, as though they had been sucked into another dimension. Nobody would believe even the story of what had happened in the bar of the seamen's pub, although a number of eye-witnesses vouched for it.

The name of the ship and the list of members of the crew are said to be kept in the secret files of the US Navy, in sealed packets. Questions from Dr Jessup were met with a blank 'No comment' by officials.

In 1957 he was once more summoned to the Office of Naval Research in Washington and asked whether he knew who was responsible for the marginal notes to the copy of his book that had been sent to Admiral Bennett. Dr Jessup did not know, as the Navy Office was well aware. The marginal notes are said to be concerned with questions about displacement in space and time, and the problem of achieving total invisibility, as proposed in the 'Philadelphia Experiment'.

The whole affair smacked so much of mystery-mongering that some scientists were beginning to ask questions and, since official authorities refused information, they turned to Dr Jessup for his opinion. A short time afterwards – at 6.20 a.m. on 20th April 1957 – the astrophysicist was found dead in his parked car, near Coral Gables, Florida. Doctors signed the death certificate as suicide; but nobody who knew Dr Jessup personally would believe in the verdict. Apart from the US Government, he was the only person who knew the secret of the dematerialization of the ship and its crew. Dr Jessup's death is regarded by many people as part of the unsolved mystery of the 'Philadelphia Experiment'.

Whether or not this story is founded on fact is very difficult to decide. In the main, people are much more inclined to look upon it as questionable and to negate it out of hand. The scientific explanations produced to bolster up the experiment are obscure and not particularly convincing. None the less, a good many highly reputable people have taken it seriously.

The 'cloak of invisibility' has probably always been one of humanity's favourite dreams. Perhaps that is the reason why interest in the question has never died down.

If Allende was really 'touched', it is all the more curious that he managed to keep his 'canard' alive for so many years. And for this, if for no other reason, it seems worth while to repeat the story – whether it really happened or not.

9. Contact with Extra-Terrestrial Life

> Before things happen we ascribe other causes
> to them than after they have taken place.
>
> F. Nietzsche

Not so very long ago it was believed that the planet Earth was unique in the universe. Our present knowledge, however, shows very clearly that we are nothing out of the ordinary in the cosmic infinity. And the possibility of the existence of extra-terrestrial forms of life can no longer be questioned. In fact, it seems probable that we must reckon with there being extra-terrestrial civilizations whose scientific achievements are far beyond our own.

Speculations of this sort have given a new impetus to interest in the possibility of making interstellar contacts. In Russia, for example, a 17-metre radio-telescope has been built for the sole purpose of listening-in systematically to fifty stars that are relatively near us, in order to catch possible broadcasts from extra-terrestrial civilizations. And in America, 'Project Ozma' at the beginning of the 1960s has been followed by 'Project Cyclops', which will carry on the search with the help of radio-telescopes and highly sensitive 'super-computers'.

It is not known when the idea of making interstellar contacts was first mooted. But even one who lived as long ago as Thales of Miletus (636–546 BC) suggested that stars might be other worlds. His pupil, Anaximander, then put forward the notion that there might be innumerable other worlds, some of which would die, while others would be born. Plutarch (AD 46–125) looked upon the moon as a miniature earth, its hills and valleys populated by demons.

The means by which contact should be made, however,

have been seriously considered only in recent times. The famous mathematician, C. F. Gauss (1777–1855), suggested laying out a huge right-angled triangle in Siberia by planting lines of trees. The Austrian astronomer J. J. von Littrow (1781–1840), again, recommended that geometrically aligned canals should be dug in the Sahara, and lit up at night with kerosene. And the Frenchman Ch. Gros proposed sending signals to Mars during sunlight hours by using a super-dimensional mirror.

Suggestions became more realistic with the discovery of radio waves. One of the pioneers here was that unique genius Nikola Tesla (1856–1943) who claimed, shortly after the installation of his electrostatic laboratory at Colorado Springs, USA, to have picked up signals of interstellar origin. And his contemporary, Thomas Edison (1847–1931), described similar phenomena. Both were attacked, sneered at and ridiculed by sceptics, and said no more on the subject.

If for no other reason, recent sensational reports of 'biological signals' from extra-terrestrial life should be examined with greater impartiality. The fact that these signals were recorded by chance makes them all the more interesting, in that they were not – as might have been expected – electro-magnetic impulses, but call-signs of biological origin.

It would seem that a first contact has now been established with some extra-terrestrial intelligence. The latest developments in California suggest that something absolutely staggering is happening. The signals were reported by the Ecola Institute in San Bernardino, California, a body that specializes in environmental and certain forms of space research.

These mysterious impulses were recorded for the first time on 29th October 1971. From what L. George Lawrence, the Head of the Ecola Institute, has said, the impulses came on lengths outside those of the electro-magnetic spectrum. They were not, therefore, recorded by radio-telescope, but by another type of apparatus.

Lawrence had been hoping to show by experiments

carried out in the Mojave Desert, that plants emitted biological impulses. The Ecola Institute had developed highly
sensitive apparatuses for the purpose, including an organic
transformer that would catch biological radiations, transform these into sound-waves, amplify them, and then
record them on tape.

During an interval in the work, it happened that the
instruments were trained on the constellation Ursa Major
(the Great Bear) for about half an hour. In spite of this,
impulses were recorded that Lawrence identified as of
biological origin.

Since he had screened the receivers against every known
type of radiation from the electro-magnetic spectrum by
means of a Faraday tube, the unexpected impulses could
not possibly originate from this particular field. And their
constant repetition excluded chance. The sender had to
be sought at a distance that man, with his present technical
facilities, cannot bridge. Lawrence was staggered.

But his analytical mind obliged him to look for possible
faults in the apparatus. He switched over to the non-
stop tone of his machine, thinking that some electrical
failure might be responsible for the unexpected sounds;
or that the speed was wrong for the replay. He listened
tensely.

His eye caught the outline of the 6-inch refractive telescope with its attached Faraday tube. In the dim light it
stood out above the complex of optical and electronic
apparatus like a pointing finger.

He checked the direction of the telescope and repeatedly
compared his calculations with an astronomical chart.
There was no reason whatever for doubt. The instruments
were functioning perfectly. The strong and continuous
signals he heard were coming from the direction of Ursa
Major – signals from life on another world.

Lawrence was dumbfounded at the idea of interstellar
communication by means of biological signals. It was
maddening to think that contact had perhaps been established millions of years ago on a biological wave-length,
and here we were, wasting our time on radio-telescopes in

the electro-magnetic range.

The study of radiations from vegetable life was taken seriously only after February 1966, when Cleve Backster, one of the leading experts in lie-detection, discovered the psycho-galvanic reactions of plants. He was watering some plants that were attached to a polygraph (lie-detector), and was intending only to watch his galvanometer to find out how long it took for the moisture to reach the leaves.

Two electrodes, one on each side of a leaf, were charged with a low-voltage current, and these set in motion a 'writer' on a roll of paper by means of a galvanometer. Emotional impulses influence the electrical characteristics of an organism and cause a direct and immediate reaction in the 'writer'.

Backster was enormously surprised to find that the polygraph registered the same sort of reaction as it did when human beings were under great emotional stress.

On an impulse, Backster thought about burning a leaf. But before he had time to strike the match – practically as the idea came into his head – the needle on the polygraph jerked wildly. An astounding fact emerged, that *no* reaction was recorded when he only *pretended* he was going to burn a plant without really intending to do so. Reactions were noted only when the life of a plant was threatened seriously.

In a series of carefully controlled experiments Backster subsequently verified that plants and animals both registered similar reactions.

The polygraph reacted even when different forms of life were threatened. Philodendron plants, for instance, reacted to the death of shrimps in boiling water – even when they were some distance away, in another room and separated by closed doors – in much the same fashion as human beings would if they were faced by something horrifying.

This made Backster wonder whether dying cells perhaps sent out warning signals to other – live – cells. In a series of experiments concerned with the destruction of other forms of life, it was found that the same reactions were always obtained, no matter whether they came from fruit, vegetable, amoeba, yeast or seed cells.

On the other hand, he discovered that when the experiment with shrimps was repeated a number of times, the reactions grew progressively less acute. From this, Backster argued that some sort of adaptability or possibly even a kind of memory was developed; that the plants reached a stage when they 'realized' that the death of the shrimps did not affect their own well-being and was therefore no threat to them.

If plants are exposed to extremes of threat or danger, they simply 'faint', as Backster discovered by chance. A Canadian physiologist was anxious to see for herself the reaction of a galvanometer to radiations from plants. The very first plant showed no reaction whatever. The galvanometer recorded an almost straight line.

Backster was speechless.

Then an idea occurred to him. He asked the visitor whether her research included damage to plants. It transpired that all the plants she worked with were roasted in an oven, to establish their dry weight. . . . The plants did not recover from the shock until three-quarters of an hour later, after the visitor had left.

Further experiments showed that plants and those who look after them stand in a close relationship that is not affected even by absence. This was demonstrated in an automatic survey carried out with the help of exactly synchronized stop-watches. By this means, Backster was able to prove that his plants reacted to his thoughts, no matter where he happened to be. He was able to register an immediate positive reaction from his plants to a sudden decision to return to New York from New Jersey – a distance of some fifteen miles.

In the same way he succeeded in checking the reaction of plants over a distance of more than 1,000 miles, with the help of some plants belonging to a friend. She was making a round trip of America, covering something like 3,000 miles, and at every landing or take-off her plants reacted to the anxieties of their owner.

It is not as yet known which is the source of energy that transmits human thoughts or emotions to a plant. Backster has tried isolating plants in a Faraday tube or in a lead container. But no form of screening was able to sever the link between man and plant. Backster argued therefore that this form of radiation must lie outside the electro-magnetic spectrum; that its speed is much greater than that of light and is unaffected by time or space.

An absolutely sensational experiment of this kind was carried out successfully by the electro-engineer and inventor Paul Sauvin. By means of a special apparatus of his own design he sent a mental order to a philodendron plant that stood on the windowsill of his laboratory, 15 kilometres from his home. When the philodendron received the order from Sauvin, it emitted a signal that switched on the ignition key of a car standing in the laboratory's car park, and started the engine.

Sauvin's thought-transference and its receipt by the plant were recorded *at the same instant* and simultaneously, by the short-wave radio station at Boulder, Colorado, 2,000 kilometres away.

The results of these experiments, which were corroborated at a number of research stations all over the world, show that biological transmission of energy is in many respects greatly superior to conventional electro-magnetic waves for purposes of communication.

If, therefore, 'biological waves' really prove to be much faster than light-waves, it would be obvious why extra-terrestrial forms of life had decided on this system for making contact; for if they were separated by enormous distances in the universe, they would use a form of energy for making contact that would cover such distances with practically no loss of time – instantaneously.

Remembering this, it is no longer a matter for surprise that Lawrence should have picked up biological signals from another world on that October evening in 1971.

The importance attached by the scientific world to Lawrence's sound-recordings is shown by the fact that the tapes have been deposited in the scientific archives of the Smithsonian Institution, Washington, DC, as evidence of an important historical landmark.

Evaluation of the tapes has not yet been possible, because the code has not yet been broken. Meanwhile, more of these strange signals have been recorded; and the Ecola Institute is continuing research on its remarkable discovery.

An independent confirmation of the phenomenon by other researchers would no doubt be welcomed by L. George Lawrence.

10. Space-Probe from Epsilon Boötes

. . . Some day, in the far, far distant future,
I shall be understood.

Morgenstern

A space-probe from outer space has entered our solar system.

This sensational piece of news was given by Duncan A. Lunan, a twenty-seven-year-old Scottish astronomer. He discovered that certain delayed echoes of radio signals transmitted from the earth at regular intervals might be interpreted as a sort of code.

According to Lunan, a space-probe from Epsilon Boötes arrived in our solar system about 13,000 years ago and has been trying to make contact with us by reflecting our signals in the form of delayed echoes.

The first allusion to a space-probe occurred in 1960 in an article in *Nature* by Professor R. N. Bracewell, of the Radio Astronomy Institute, Stanford University, USA. The existence of such signals was, however, already known to Tesla, and he, too, surmised that they originated from an extra-terrestrial space-probe. Bracewell was of the opinion that, if advanced civilizations exist within our stellar system at a distance of 100 light-years or more, unmanned space-probes would be the likeliest means for them to attempt to make contact with us. It might be, he thought, that a probe entering our solar system would intercept our radio signals and reflect them back to us; they would appear as echoes, with a delay varying from seconds to minutes, like those reported by Tesla in the 1920s. If we were to re-transmit these echoes, the probe would 'know' that it had made contact with some form of intelligent life. 'Would it be surprising,' Bracewell wondered, 'if the beginning of such a communication turned out to be a television picture of one of the constellations?'

Lunan's discoveries are certainly thrilling; for he succeeded in transcribing the signals with delayed echoes to make a simple graphical diagram. The resultant figure showed the constellations of the northern hemisphere. The positions of the stars are by now slightly different from those shown on the graph, and the binary-star Epsilon Boötes comes in the wrong place.

By using astronomical measuring techniques, Lunan has now reckoned that his diagram gave an accurate representation of the skies as they were 13,000 years ago. From this, he has deduced that the space-probe arrived in our solar system at that time and was programmed to make contact with some other intelligence by echoing in a distinctive way any radio signals it picked up.

The obvious misplacing of Epsilon Boötes was, Lunan thinks, probably intentional, in order to draw attention to it as the home base of the probe.

John Stoneley, of the London *Enquirer*, says on this point: 'Lunan's discovery is simply stupendous. The chances are 10,000 : 1 against the likelihood that the delayed echoes would produce a map of the stars. This extra-terrestrial space-probe must be an incomparably advanced sort of computer. As soon as the existence of the probe is definitely proved, we should "interrogate" it. If it turns out to be the proof that contact has been established with some other intelligence, it might lead to the release of information from its certainly immense store of data.'

Meanwhile members of the British Interplanetary Society are proposing to send radio signals into space, with the special purpose of getting on to the track of this mysterious probe, hoping thereby possibly to find an explanation for the radio echoes which have been heard at intervals ever since 1927.

The first accounts of long-delayed echoes were given as the result of experiments by two Americans, Taylor and Young. As early as 1927, while searching for echoes from the ionosphere, they had discovered other echoes that undoubtedly originated at a distance of between 2,900 and 10,000 kilometres. The periodicity of the echoes was one hundredth part of a second; and the distances corresponded pretty nearly with the extent of the inner Van Allen Belt. (A belt of radiation surrounding the earth, and containing a very large number of cosmic particles.) This would permit of a natural explanation.

In December 1927, Professor Carl Störmer, of Oslo, happened to meet Jorgen Hals, one of the engineers at the Philips Laboratories in Eindhoven, Holland, and discussed the Taylor-Young experiments with him. It appeared that Hals had observed echoes with three seconds' delay to signals sent out over the Philips exploratory transmitter PCJJ. Hals believed that these echoes came from the moon.

On 28th October 1928, Dr van der Pol, of the Philips Laboratories, then arranged for a series of short impulses to be transmitted every thirty seconds between eight and nine o'clock one morning in quick succession – a total of 120 impulses. The delays between the emission of the impulses and the echoes were 8, 11, 15, 8, 13, 3, 8, 8, 8, 12, 15, 13, 8, and 8 seconds. The echoes came back faintly but perfectly audibly. The most important thing was, however, the fact that they all came on the same wavelength.

Duncan Lunan commented: 'If these echoes originated from a space-probe, it is simply tragic that they happened to be received at a time when they would as a matter of course be attributed to some natural phenomenon.'

And in Morrison's opinion it is even more unfortunate that this hypothetical space-probe did not attract attention to itself by some 'unmistakable characteristic'. – 'In normal circumstances, anyone designing a space-probe would hardly reckon with the idea that an echo after a three-second delay could be mistaken for some natural phenomenon.'

At the beginning of the 1950s, when theories about the

possibility of extra-terrestrial echo-signals were no longer necessarily regarded as fairy tales, it was decided to make another attempt at investigating the echoes. This time observers came to the conclusion that it really must be an extra-terrestrial communication-probe that announced itself from time to time. It was presumed that its purpose was to search for any form of intelligent life in our solar system, and to re-transmit radio transmissions from here to its own distant home-planet. From these new investigations it was also found that the echo-signals of the exploratory probe were intercepted only at intervals.

Then, on 4th September 1953, at half past three in the afternoon, something really uncanny happened. C. W. Bradley, watching television in London, quite suddenly and unconnected with anything else, saw the American programme-signal KLEE-TV on his screen. During that month and again later, the same letters appeared on the screens of Atlantic Electronics Ltd, at Lancaster, in England.

Of course television transmissions from overseas do not necessarily give cause for anxiety, but in this case the programme-signal KLEE-TV had been transmitted three years *previously* from Houston, in Texas, and never again. It was replaced by the signal KPRC-TV in July 1950. Thereafter the letters KLEE-TV were never transmitted by any station on earth.

No really satisfactory explanation was ever given for this curious incident, although attempts were made to solve the enigma by various theories, ranging from plasma clouds (ionized gas) – that might for some unknown reason have stored up the signals for a long time in order to release them later – to a hypothetical extra-terrestrial space-probe.

It may well be that Lunan's conclusions will enable us to resolve the secret of the mysterious echoes, and that there really is an unknown space-probe in our system. It would appear to be about as far away from us as the moon, and may have started from the twin star Epsilon Boötes – itself 103 light-years distant – with the intention of making contact with us if at all possible . . . A probe launched by an unknown intelligence, over 13,000 years ago, in order to look for some other form of life . . . sent by beings living on a planet in orbit round one of the twin stars we name Epsilon Boötes. . . .

Since these particular binary stars are something like twelve milliard kilometres apart, each might be surrounded by a number of planets permanently in orbit.

Lunan, it seems, is fully convinced that the inhabitants of the Epsilon Boötes system were not actuated by purely dispassionate scientific thirst for knowledge when they sent their space-probe on its 103-light-years' journey.

'They are looking for a new home,' he believes, 'and no doubt the whole genus is interested in this space project, and is prepared to register success or failure at the end of the 13,000 years.'

Opinions might differ on this point.

We, too, have sent a space-probe on an interstellar journey – the Pioneer-F-Probe. It was launched in February 1972, and will leave our solar system after sending back information about the asteroid belt and the planet Jupiter – always supposing that everything goes according to plan.

In the course of its journey it might cover a distance of nearly 3,000 light-years in the Milky Way, taking about a hundred million years to do so. But the journey was not undertaken for the purpose of finding another planet as a new home for human beings. A gold-plated aluminium plaque, showing naked humans – male and female – and some binary mathematical symbols, was affixed to the probe, with the intention of giving a possible discoverer some idea of whence and by whom it was despatched into the cosmos.

The chances that it may be picked up by some extra-terrestrial beings are really very considerable. In our galaxy alone there are milliards of stars with planets that could support life – six milliard stars with habitable planets, according to the most conservative expert estimates. So it may be that in the far distant future our probe may reveal its secrets to another civilization 103 light-years away from us. If it travelled at a speed of about 50,000 kilometres an

J.I.   E hour, it would still take something like 530,000 years to get there.

One wonders: will the human race still be in existence then?

11. In the Beginning was Energy

*Nature has no system; it has, it is life, that streams
from an unknown centre to an unknowable
periphery. The study of Nature may therefore be
carried on unceasingly; it may be taken in detail
or studied as a whole in length and depth.*

Goethe

The realization that inhabited worlds may exist all over
the cosmos is due largely to the tremendous revolution
that has taken place during the last few years in our
knowledge of astronomy.

Astronomy is probably one of the oldest of the sciences
and, although its origins are generally attributed to the
Babylonians, there are indications that, long before their
day, it had been studied far more deeply and with much
greater perspicuity.

Quite recently, for example, an immensely ancient astronomical chart was discovered near Poiré in La Vendée; to
put it more accurately, it should be described as a pre-
historic block of stone with a number of interesting designs
engraved on the side facing the sky.

Dr Marcel Baudouin, the French scholar, believed –
rightly as was afterwards proved – that the designs were
maps of the constellations. He had a cast made of the
stone and had it minutely examined by various learned institutions, which ultimately endorsed his conclusions. Dr
Baudouin's star-chart – named 'Pierre de Merlière' – closely
resembles the oldest representation of the signs of the
Zodiac made in ancient China and called the 'Standard of
Heaven'.

On this French stone, a right circular spiral runs towards
the centre, ending at this point in a depression. This is the
cardinal point of the chart, and represents the position of
the observer. From here, two small furrows branch off

in different directions. One runs towards the north and ends in a cross. Above and below the transverse bar of the cross four small indentations have been cut. Notches of various sizes beside these represent the constellation of the Great Bear. It is known today that the Great Bear stood for the meridian to Stone Age man.

The second furrow runs from the central depression in a north-westerly direction. At the winter equinox this line marks the position of the rising sun. In the south-west section of the stone is yet another shallow round depression, with two concentric circles; this indicates the summer solstice.

Careful study disclosed a number of other signs; and it finally proved possible to work out, according to the position of the signs, the date at which the constellations would have been seen in the night sky in these latitudes. From this it was reckoned that the chart must be 8,500 years old. All over Europe, from Spain to the Ukraine, bones and stones have been discovered, marked with dots and lines – pictures going back to 35,000 BC. . . . According to the American scientist, Alexander Marshak, these designs record the results of lunar observations.

Between the years 2000 and 1700 BC agriculture and cattle-breeding were carried on by Stone Age men in England. These people are said to have been backward in comparison with those living under Mediterranean cultures during the same era, yet it is from this period that Stonehenge dates – that mysterious megalithic monument, raised high on Salisbury Plain in South-West England.

Standing stones, up to 16 or 20 feet high, weighing forty or more tons apiece, are ranged in a closed circle, with a gap in one place that might have been an entrance. Lintels still remain in position, joining some of the uprights in pairs. Around this circle is a ditch as well as another circle containing fifty-six holes, known as the Aubrey Holes (*after the eighteenth-century antiquary who explored them*). The ground-plan shows that it was designed in concentric circles; the diameter of the entire area is about 370 feet.

Within the first circle are forty-nine trilithons in the form of a horse-shoe. An inner section consists of somewhat smaller stone blocks, also laid out in the form of a horse-shoe. In the centre is a single large stone. The longitudinal axis of the larger horse-shoe points North-West, and is prolonged to form a sort of stone avenue.

Professor Gerald S. Hawkins, the astronomer, was told on one occasion when he was on a visit in the neighbourhood that at the summer solstice it was possible to watch the sun rise over a large stone at the end of the Avenue (*the Heel Stone*). He proved this for himself, and further study convinced him that the Avenue was part of a complex observatory.

In order to minimize time-consuming research and generally to hasten the process of the study, Hawkins installed a computer. He fed this with key facts about Stonehenge and with astronomical data.

The astonishing result showed that Stonehenge was not only a complex observatory, giving information about solstices and equinoxes, solar and lunar eclipses, but was at the same time a calendar – that, in fact, Stonehenge was itself a sort of computer.

How the gigantic blocks of stone reached Stonehenge and how they were put in position remains a mystery. The so-called bluestones, for example, derive from the Prescelly Hills in Pembrokeshire, some 250 miles away.

Another notable sight in England, a prehistoric landmark of titanic proportions, is to be seen in the neighbourhood of Glastonbury in Somerset. An immense planetarium extends over something like five and three-quarter square miles, its mounds and artificial water-courses representing the signs of the Zodiac. It is a vast astral chart, that can really only be seen properly from an aircraft. It is older than the great pyramid.

A picture – drawn to scale – of our solar system, and dating from pre-historic days, was discovered in a South American cave.

And on a fragment of pottery dug up from the Kujundshik mound on the site of ancient Nineveh, was found the record of an arithmetical calculation that ran into fifteen figures: 195,955,200,000,000 was the end result. It came from Sumeria, probably the oldest known of the advanced civilizations of man, alleged to be co-eval with the Creation. They wrote 'books' on clay tablets, and had an amazing knowledge of mathematics and astronomy. Their calculation of the moon's orbit differed from ours by no more than 0.4 seconds.

How was that possible?

The movements of the planets Venus, Mars and Jupiter are given absolutely accurately in the 4,000-year-old cuneiform records of Babylonian astronomers. Even the positional changes of Jupiter's four moons are described, although these are not visible to the naked eye. Telescopes were not invented until 1608, by Hans Lippershey in Holland.

How on earth did the Babylonians manage to do what they did?

The Creation began with a mist – a cloud – a cloud of dust, according to the *Popul Vuh*, the sacred book of the Mayas of Central America. And Chinese scholars realized three thousand years ago that the earth must be round; while Europeans, whose scientific education was only achieved much later, still thought of the earth as a flat disc.

Some 2,500 years BC, when the Emperor Yao ruled in China, two court astronomers, Ho and Hi, were victims of a fatal accident. Having indulged too freely in rice-wine, they omitted to mention an eclipse of the sun which, according to the terms of their employment, they should have notified. For being drunk while on duty and failing to carry out their contract, they were relieved of their posts by decapitation.

The Indian Vedas, too, described life on other celestial bodies far removed from the earth.

The famous philosopher and mathematician, Pythagoras of Samos, realized, as early as 570 BC, that the earth is round and floats freely in space.

Yet later, in the darkness of the Middle Ages, the Church

refused, for egocentric reasons, to admit any but the Ptolemaic system, according to which the earth was the fixed centre round which everything else revolved.

It was not until the time of Nicholas Copernicus (1473–1543) that the situation was rectified. He sent the earth and the other planets revolving round the sun again, basing his views upon those of Aristarchus of Samos (320–250 BC) who had in his day maintained that the sun was the central point for the surrounding planets.

Some 2,500 years ago Anaxagoras (500–428 BC) had actually gone a step farther. He said that besides our world, other worlds must be capable of supporting life.

Over two thousand years later Giordano Bruno (1547–1600), a Dominican monk, was burnt at the stake, for having dared to suggest that other worlds besides our own must be in existence.

Democritus (460 BC–370 BC), who first formulated the atomic theory, spoke of the birth and death of worlds and thought that some of them were suitable for living creatures. In his opinion, the Milky Way was simply a collection of distant stars.

Heraclitus of Pontus (388–310 BC), too, saw every star as the centre of a planetary system.

About 120 BC, in the book *Huai Nan Tzu*, the Chinese described the origin of the worlds as deriving from primeval matter in revolution.

And in 65 BC Greek astronomers were already using computers. Sponge divers found some corroded metal parts near the island of Antikythera about the year 1900. The complicated remains of mechanism and dials were examined by Professor Derek Solla Price in 1959, and according to fragmentary inscriptions it proved possible to date the odds and ends at about 65 BC. Professor Solla Price recognized it as a highly developed calculating machine that was used for representing and interpreting the movements of planets, the sun and the moon.

No more than fragmentary remains of the distant past have reached us across the millennia; but even these scraps surpass every expectation.

We cannot tell how many civilizations having an immense knowledge of science and metaphysics have vanished without a trace, since only myths and legends tell of them.

No less tragic are the losses that have occurred in the more recent past – for example, the Great Library of Alexandria, to name only one among many. Its manuscript rolls, containing irreplaceable treasures of learning, went up in flames in 47 BC. To say nothing of the innumerable documents of inestimable value that are in 'safe keeping' in the archives of the Vatican, and are therefore inaccessible to scholars. Even the number of books and papers confiscated by the Inquisition simply because they could not be reconciled with the dogmas of the Church . . . Centuries of oppression resulted in retrogression rather than advancement of learning.

Yet, despite every discouragement, scholars succeeded, although slowly, in re-discovering lost knowledge. Thus Johannes Kepler (1571–1631) was able to make use of the papers left by the Danish astronomer Tycho Brahe (1546–1601) to demonstrate the eliptical track of the planets round the sun and of the moon round the earth. Kepler's laws became standard in astronomy.

Galileo Galilei (1643–1727) built a telescope on the model of Lippershey's, and managed to see mountains on the moon, Jupiter's satellites, and sunspots. But although he was a passionate advocate of the teachings of Copernicus, he was forced by the Inquisition to abjure this 'false doctrine'.

Isaac Newton (1643–1727), the great English scientist, was the first to formulate the laws of gravity; he invented the reflector-telescope, and did considerable research into the nature of light.

The greatest of modern pioneers in the study of astronomy, however, was surely Friedrich Wilhelm Herschel (1738–1822). Having started life as a musician, he suddenly, at the age of thirty-five, decided to devote his attention to astronomy after reading a book on the subject. It is impossible to describe all his work here, but he made the study of the heavens his main object throughout his long life, working with a telescope designed by himself, that can to this day compete with the best. He wrote an enormous number of memoranda describing his researches; and in 1780/81 he discovered the planet Uranus.

In 1846 he was followed by the French astronomer Urbain Jean Joseph Leberrier (1811–1877), who calculated that there must certainly be at least one other planet in our solar system; and this planet – Neptune – was finally discovered by Johann Gottfried Galle (1812–1910), working at the Berlin observatory. Finally, the planet that, so far as we know at present, is the most distant from the sun – Pluto – was located by the American, Clyde William Tombaugh, who was born in 1906. More recently, however, it has been thought that one or possibly two more planets are likely to exist beyond Pluto.

As recently as the end of the last century, astronomers were concerned exclusively with our solar system and the evolution of the stars. Other galaxies (stellar systems) were then still considered to be incidental nebulae within our Milky Way. Although the philosopher Immanuel Kant (1729–1804) had already suggested that they were *not* nebulae, nor within our Milky Way, but were similar large remote stellar systems, the problem was not resolved until an American astronomer, E. P. Hubble (1889–1953), came on the scene.

By using the Mount Wilson 2½-metre reflector-telescope Hubble succeeded in 1926 in resolving into individual stars the outlying parts of the Andromeda nebula and other stellar systems.

There are galaxies of all sizes all over the universe. Our Milky Way, for instance, consists of something like 150 milliard stars. By the use of the spectroscope it has now been shown that galaxies flee from one another, as can be seen from their red shift. In the same way that the whistle of a locomotive sounds deeper as it gets farther away, so the colour of astronomical bodies changes as they retreat from us. The colour shifts towards the red side of the optical spectrum, an effect which is the visual equivalent of deepening sound; for, like the lowest audible sound-waves, the vibrations of the red light-waves move the most slowly.

Hubble now discovered that, as the galaxies moved farther away, their red shift also increased. That is to say that, the more distant galaxies are, the faster they are moving. In other words, their speed increases proportionally to their distance. And this led to the concept of the expanding universe.

In 1970, the most remote object within our range was located at the utterly unimaginable distance of twelve milliard light-years. (Light waves travel 9,463 billion kilometres in a single year – that is, one light-year.)

This far-distant object is a quasar (quasi stellar source of radiation), which has been designated OH 471. It has been calculated that this quasar is moving away from us at a speed of about 91% of the speed of light – about 270,000 kilometres per second.

Quasars were first discovered in 1963. They look like dots, almost invisible; but they caused great excitement when it turned out that they emitted tremendously powerful radio waves. How they produce their terrific energy is still obscure; because, although the average quasar has the illuminating power of hundreds of galaxies, it is, in comparison with the size of any one galaxy, very, very small.

About six milliard years ago our solar system was condensed from a swirling cloud of gas. But the particular radio wave that reaches us today from Quasar OH 471 was emitted just twice as long ago, that is, twelve milliard years.

The universe: '. . . shows us both past and present. Light takes thousands, millions, and sometimes milliards of years to convey the picture of its source to us on earth. Yet this picture, which is only the image of the living past, helps us to grasp the present, that is no less dynamic and wonderful. To look at the sky is to look across time, and shows the history of stars in all stages of development.

'But what is happening in the universe today will not be visible on earth until long-after humanity has died out . . .' says Victor Ambarzumjan, head of the astrophysical observatory at Bjurakan, in Armenia.

One would expect the increasing expansion of the universe to result in a correspondingly increasing vacuum. And if we could trace the expansion backwards, speeding it up, we should see the galaxies approaching one another, and should observe the cosmos growing noticeably smaller and denser, until the point was reached where all the galaxies met and were condensed into a single gigantic super-atom.

This, at any rate, is how the Abbé Georges LeMaître, the Belgian mathematician and physicist sees it. In 1927 he came to the conclusion that milliards of years ago – about fifteen milliards, it is now thought – the universe was compressed into a single primordial atom in the form of elementary particles.

Of unimaginable density, milliards of times surpassing the density of water, this super-atom must have had an absolute temperature of many milliard degrees. It was probably composed of neutrons compressed to the ultimate (neutronium). Then, about fifteen milliard years ago, it burst in a mighty explosion.

A 'big Bang', the astrophysicist G. Gamov called it in 1948 in a thesis based on the LeMaître theory. The fragments resulting from the Big Bang were hurled in every direction, eventually to be re-condensed into galaxies. It is thought that the flight of galaxies observed at present originated from the initial explosion.

This postulate is now generally agreed to be correct, although it contains certain weaknesses and contradictions. Not even the reason for the explosion can be given satisfactorily. Although the theory accounts for the beginning of the expansion of the universe, it entirely fails to explain the origins of energy and matter. Moreover, the problem of time is neglected. The absolute beginning of time is arbitrarily fixed at the moment of the explosion, on the assumption that time did not exist in the primeval atom. But how is the process leading to the explosion – or, rather, to the expansion – to be explained without reference to time? Who was it that pressed the button to release the cosmic bomb?

Besides, the expansion – speed of flight of the Big Bang fragments – contradicts the laws of physics and gravity as we know them.

Some scientists have tried to get round the question as to what, how, or where was the primeval atom before the original explosion occurred, by suggesting that the matter composing the atom had been dispersed all over the cosmos in the form of a great cloud; this had contracted, and finally condensed into the primeval atom. Why contraction took place is not explained convincingly. And the question of the origin of matter remains open.

Another conjecture indicates that in x milliard years the expansion we recognize today will come to a halt, the process of contraction will resume until maximum condensation is reached, and this will once more give place to expansion – producing an ever-recurrent rhythmic cycle.

Professor Sandage, of the Mount Wilson Observatory, believes that one such cycle of expansion and contraction takes eighty-two milliard years.

Ever since Paul Dirac, the British physicist, advanced the theory that for every atom there is an anti-atom – a sort of looking-glass reflection of matter – speculation has been rife about the possible place of anti-matter in the universe. Soon after Dirac's proposition was put forward, the first anti-particle – the positron – was discovered. It is like an electron, but differs from it in having a positive electrical charge, and rotating in the opposite direction.

Recently two Soviet scientists, Valentin I. Petruchin and Vladimir I. Rykalin, succeeded in producing the atomic nuclei of a new kind of anti-matter. They bombarded aluminium foil with proton rays (rays from the nuclei of hydrogen atoms), that had been speeded up by the accelerator in Serpukhov, south of Moscow, to equal a voltage of seventy million electrons.

The impact of these particles upon the nuclei of the aluminium atoms caused, among other things, the formation of atomic nuclei composed of two anti-neutrons and one anti-proton. These are anti-tritium atomic nuclei, complementary to the atomic nuclei of the radio-active hydrogen isotope, Tritium.

Yu. D. Prokoshkin has reported that the Russians produced anti-helium nuclei at Serpukhov, as long as three years earlier.

Now that the existence of anti-matter has been demonstrated, it is thought possible that there may be not only anti-stars, whole anti-galaxies, but actually an anti-universe.

Of course, if matter were to collide with anti-matter – stars with anti-stars, for example – the degree of mutual destruction would be utterly inconceivable. All that would remain would be an incalculable amount of unrestrained energy. Atom-bomb explosions would be as nothing in comparison.

It appears now that some experts are of the opinion that quasars and radio-galaxies, both of which emit enormous amounts of radio-energy, may be explainable as the result of collisions between matter and anti-matter. But up to the present there is no way of differentiating between, say, galaxies and anti-galaxies.

To visualize an anti-planetary system, with anti-humanity living on an anti-earth, is an attractive idea – but only as long as man and anti-man don't shake hands . . . Big Bang!

The Russian scientist A. Sakharov is inclined to believe that our universe was actually born of an anti-universe that disintegrated twenty or thirty milliard years ago in an explosion. Originally, Sakharov thinks, this universe consisted mainly of anti-matter; the explosion was caused by condensation at a very high temperature, and in the course of disintegration more matter than anti-matter was produced. Our universe was formed of the resultant particles of matter.

In stark contradiction to these explosion-theories (the evolutionary theory) is that of Fred Hoyle, H. Bondi and T. Gold.

Hoyle favours the view that the universe is unchangeable in time and space; that it has never been a primeval atom nor will ever become one in the future. Even if we were to go back milliards of years into the past, the constitution of the galaxies would be found to be exactly the same as it is at present – different galaxies no doubt, but their general distribution unchanged.

This so-called 'steady state' theory argues on the assumption that matter in the universe remains constant. To make up for the galaxies fleeing from one another, proportionate quantities of new matter – new galaxies – will come into existence in order to preserve the state of equilibrium.

Since, according to Hoyle's theory, matter (in the form of hydrogen atoms) develops, as it were, from 'nothing' but seems thereby to violate the law of the conservation of energy, it has been vigorously attacked.

Leaving Hoyle's 'nothing' out of account, and substituting instead 'something', this 'something' may be regarded as a sort of universal creative energy.

Within this field of energy, tension would cause the formation of sub-atomic particles, which would in due course unite to build complex structures. Matter would, in fact, be nothing other than concentrated or materialized energy.

The propensity of this universal field of energy to create ever more complex structures would explain why life and eventually consciousness were evolved. This would make everything a part of the field of energy, of elementary force. And if one should question where it all began, the answer would be that the origin must be sought in this ultimate creative force, in a universe that created itself.

For thousands of years, man regarded the universe with awe, as a reliable clockwork system, functioning with mathematical accuracy. Nowadays the universe is known to be a turbulent, highly dramatic, incalculable play of forces. Astrophysicists and cosmologists slip like divers into eternal darkness. They are time-travellers, feeling their way, as through a time-tunnel, past cosmic vortices, atrophied galaxies, ever-luminous sources of radiance, invisible suns, whose output of energy exceeds 100,000 times that of our own sun. They will happen upon quasars and quasi-quasars – recently discovered mystery stars that make no impact on the visual spectrum of wave-lengths; they will meet variable cosmic luminaries – pulsars – as well as 'white dwarfs', cold, dead cosmic bodies that have no need of internal radiation. And on their way into the milliards of years past, they may come within the orbit of the time-less 'black holes', that swallow up matter, through a gravitational abyss, into everlasting darkness.

These black holes have given rise to a whole series of speculations to explain their origin. It is generally accepted nowadays that a star condenses from a nebula. The core heats up, and the forces of gravity cause it to shrink. The process of changing hydrogen into helium (hydrogen fusion) begins as soon as a certain temperature is reached.

When the force of the nuclear impulse is exhausted, a star shrivels into a 'white dwarf' – as our sun will do in about six milliard years.

In the case of larger stars, exceeding 1.2 times the mass of our sun (the Chandrasekhar limit), a super-nova explosion occurs. The interior of the star collapses to form a mass occupying only a few cubic kilometres of space, and its matter evaporates under the immense pressure to become neutronium. A neutron-star – a Pulsar – is born. A single cubic centimetre of its mass would weigh several million tons on earth. Pulsars are very probably surrounded by enormous rotating dipolar magnetic fields, the intensity of which may reach anything up to a milliard gauss. If, however, the shrunken, super-dense core of a large star is double the mass of our sun, it can survive neither as a White Dwarf nor as a Pulsar.

The shrinking process continues unceasingly. Even, it is now thought, the nuclear force is overcome by the force of gravity, and total catastrophic condensation results. Nothing is left of the star except a 'black hole' – a dark cavity, into which everything in its neighbourhood is sucked by the force of gravity and swallowed up.

Where does it all go? It may be that it is crushed and totally obliterated. Some think that it leaves our universe altogether, to reappear in another universe. But who can tell? Perhaps it will reappear in our own universe, in another place, at another time – as a quasar or anti-quasar?

12. Reaching for the Light

Must you light a torch to see the sun?
Wisdom of the East

It has become almost an indictable offence in scientific enquiry nowadays to ask WHY instead of HOW anything happens. And that is not unreasonable, because it simplifies things. An answer can fairly easily be found to explain WHY processes, functions, reactions and so on occur. But HOW might possibly cause embarrassment, because it could tend to introduce metaphysics – which would be unscientific. It is proposed, none the less, to put the unscientific question here: WHY did life evolve – and WHY consciousness?

The way in which life developed is nowadays believed to be known with a reasonable degree of certainty. The origin of life is closely connected with the evolution of the planet on which it occurs. And it is now regarded as a fact that planetary systems are formed from rotating nebulae.

The theory was recently confirmed by an important discovery. Astronomers observed that the luminosity of a certain cluster of stars fluctuated irregularly, notably one in the constellation Taurus (the Bull). This type of star is consequently known as T-Tauri-Variable. Everything seems to indicate that such stars are very young and that they are surrounded by nebulae which will ultimately form planets.

Attention was drawn to one of these stars, known as R-Mon, by means of infra-red astronomical observations. R-Mon is thought to be in the very earliest stage of condensation and is enveloped in a cloud of gas or dust. Its mass is roughly one-quarter that of our own planetary system. Astronomers are convinced that in R-Mon they are attending at the birth of a new planetary system.

Taking the earth as precedent, it is now believed that, as soon as a planet fulfils certain conditions, life will evolve. It must be of a certain size and, above all, must lie within a temperature zone that will promote life. In addition, its atmosphere and outer crust must contain a number of simple chemical compounds such as methane, water vapour, ammoniac, hydrogen-sulphide, hydrocarbon, etc.

The influence of ultra-violet rays, light, heat, lightning and other phenomena will cause more and more organic molecules to develop. There are infinite numbers of possible chemical mutations that, modified by atmospheric reactions, will cause the formation of an organic mixture – the primary matter – which, in addition to being the raw material of life, also contains the energy required for the formation of further compounds.

After about a milliard years, substances will evolve from this primeval matter, including nucleotids (combinations of phosphorus, nuclein bases and hydrocarbons, the latter being present especially in the nuclei of cells) and amino acids, the basic matter for the formation of albumens. These substances will unite to form macro-molecules (one macro-molecule contains 1,000 or more atoms) as long as certain relatively simple conditions exist; and from these the first cells will ultimately come into being. Since they are all contained in the primary matter – which is an amalgam of hundreds of different organic combinations and inorganic salts – they will absorb and 'digest' some of these materials; and so the first primitive step towards metabolism will have been taken.

It might be expected that these first living molecules would quickly use up existing stores of natural organic foodstuffs, and would thus put an end to life. But at this point other organisms develop that produce food by photosynthesis and so life goes on. In the process of synthesis, primitive organisms neutralize the energy of the light they absorb, thereby obtaining organic foods from inorganic substances.

A short time ago, details of a most remarkable discovery were given in the journal *Science*. Deep in the oldest sedimentary rock-strata in the Onverwacht Strata of the Barberton Highlands in South Africa, something was found among the fossils which seems to prove that photosynthesis began on the earth about 3.4 milliard years ago. Dr Keith Kvenvolden, head of the Chemical Evolution Branch of the Planetary Biology Division of the NASA Research Center in California, together with Dr J. William Schöpf and Dorothy Z. Oehler, of the University of California in Los Angeles, believe that these rocks have most probably given them the date at which originally inorganic carbon was transformed to organic carbon by means of photosynthetic organisms.

Since all life is based upon carbon, the discovery of carbon among these deposits reveals an extremely early stage in the development of life on earth. Photosynthesis brings with it an important bonus in the shape of oxygen. And the ozone-layer in the upper atmosphere is formed by the ultra-violet rays of the sun slowly transforming oxygen into ozone. This layer of ozone shields living beings from the greater part of the dangerous ultra-violet rays, while these same rays make an important contribution to life in the early stages. The first cell-structures then appear as primitive single-cellular organisms such as algae, amoebae and bacteria.

For a long time no one could suggest a reason why their development remained at a standstill for milliards of years and then quite suddenly, almost instantaneously it seems, they became multi-cellular, and have ever since continued developing to increasingly higher and more complex forms of life.

The marvel has been explained by the palaeobiologist Steven M. Stanley, of the John Hopkins University, America, in what seems an almost absurdly simple hypothesis, published in May 1973 in the 'Proceedings of the National Academy of Sciences'. His theory is based upon the ecological concept of 'cropping'.

Stanley compares the phenomenon with a meadow which, in favourable circumstances, produces only grass. If, however, instead of its being mown, sheep or goats are turned into this field to graze, a variety of weeds will soon sprout all over it, because the animals often root up the grass in bunches. So, where once nothing but grass was growing, quantities of different plants will be found.

Adapting the idea to the pre-Cambrian age (about $2\frac{1}{2}$ milliard years ago), Stanley's 'croppings' theory would mean that algae and bacteria fed on light and the primary matter, leaving practically nothing for other species. Starting from this point in time, millions of years were needed before evolution mastered its unfriendly environment – that is to say, before it became possible to make room for higher forms of life. As soon as this stage was reached, Stanley thinks, the circumscribed character of the whole system of life was changed – algae became food for beast-like organisms and in this way space became available for new species. In the course of time, variety and abundance of food contributed to the development of new genera in the animal world – and evolution was well under way.

Stanley saw a further point in favour of his theory in the behaviour of some of the blue and green algae, whose origin goes back to the earliest epochs of earth's existence. From time to time numbers of them gather into a compact mass, forming what are called stromatoliths. They can keep their own identity and avoid being 'cropped' only by retreating into salty inlets of the sea, where no other forms of life can flourish.

These are some of the theories that explain, in rough outlines, the way in which life probably started. But that still leaves the WHY an open question.

Of course, if a fundamental life-force, an essence, is postulated, the question can be answered. A creative energy, welding atoms into ever more complex structures, until at long last life develops – what other explanation would be needed?

Jacques Monod, the molecular biologist and Nobel prizewinner, reverts in his book *Le Hasard et la Necessité* Chance and Necessity) to an opinion that has surely been disproved by now – that life was created only once – one random shot, so to speak, in eternity.

Monod's gospel is: Now, at last, man knows that he is alone in the cold immensity of the universe, from which he has been thrown up by chance . . .'

What is the 'Chance' to which Monod's concept is to be ascribed? Surely to Monod's 'Necessity'. To regard life on earth as a single unique event in a universe filled with milliards of stars seems, quite simply, to be ridiculous.

Yet now as ever, the question of the descent of man remains a problem – despite Darwin (1809–1882), and despite the fact that his teaching on the origin of species and the principle of natural selection is generally accepted, although with numerous variants. His theory of natural selection implies that every living being tends naturally to minor physical changes.

Even if not as a matter of expediency – in other words, of the need for higher development – selection will proceed of itself, simply owing to the struggle for existence. Forms of life that happen to be better adapted to their environment are more viable and will therefore outlast those that are feebler. What we call higher development is, therefore, necessarily the result of natural selection.

Darwin's theory aroused interest, not only among scientists but in the general public, because he integrated man with the total development of life on earth.

The picture of biological evolution was given a finishing touch by Ernst Haeckel (1834–1919), one of the most enthusiastic supporters in Germany of Darwin's teaching. His very thorough researches brought him to realize that the process of human development was only a single episode in evolution as a whole.

He set apart this new branch of science – the history of the evolution of species (phylogeny) – from that of the individual (ontogeny). By incorporating in his theory everything that was known about embryology, anatomy, and paleontology, man – as the highest among mammals – was fitted naturally into the general system. Haeckel also investigated the faint traces of our animal forebears surviving from the darkest ages, and reconstructed human genealogy by means of a mathematically accurate formula – the biogenetic code – which he defined as a law. By this it is shown that a germ cell in the womb passes through every stage of evolution, from the first cell-division until it comes to birth. In this way Haeckel traced the development of man from the pre-Cambrian era to the present day.

A plain, straightforward process, one might suppose. But difficulties presented themselves as soon as the problem of the transition from animal to human was reached.

This first became acute in 1856, when the skeletal remains of Neanderthal man were unearthed by a Düsseldorf teacher named Fuhlrott. These bones proved to be between 80,000 and 120,000 years old – which alone was enough to arouse heated arguments about the pedigree of mankind. Quite a number of scholars at first inclined to the opinion that the remains must be those of some beast of prey; and during the last hundred years it has grown increasingly difficult to define man's pedigree with any degree of precision. The greater the number of hominid remains that are found – and especially since they date from the most various epochs of earth's history – the harder it becomes to classify them. They show as great a variety as the number of ancestors that can be reckoned in one's own family tree. And because of the increasing number of discoveries, the transition from animal to man has constantly to be back-dated.

Dr Leakey, the director of the National Research Centre for Pre-history and Palaeontology in Nairobi, now believes that he has discovered in homo habilis what is probably the only true ancestor of homo sapiens. This homo habilis is the creature most nearly resembling homo sapiens. He was dug up in Olduvai (now Tanzania), and lived about two million years ago.

According to anthropologists, our ancestors were hominids, living up trees in wooded country, like their cousin the anthropoid apes.

As a result of climatic changes, forest lands soon gave way to steppes, which required those early ancestors of ours to change their habits. The search for food at ground level became increasingly difficult and more dangerous with the growth of tall grasses on the steppes and the number of predatory animals lurking therein. The hominid was obliged to cope with all this; he had to adapt himself to the new surroundings if he were to survive. Our ancestors therefore found it necessary to accustom themselves gradually to standing on their hind legs, in order more easily to survey the environment. This freed their hands, and they began using them for new purposes: they picked up things, handled them, manipulated them, and made them into defensive weapons.

In this way, anthropologists believe, the invention of simple implements led to human development.

But even at this point contradictions are found. One question is: surely anthropoid apes, living in the same kind of surroundings, were faced with similar conditions of life – so why do they still live up trees? Why did they not develop along the same lines as man?

If the making of simple tools is supposed to have led to human development, why are chimpanzees, who also use artifacts, still chimpanzees?

Jane van Lawick Goodall, formerly secretary to Dr Leakey, spent ten years researching into the manners and customs of wild chimpanzees in Kenya. Within fourteen months she had managed gradually to overcome the animals' shyness, and to be accepted as one of themselves. She lived among them and so was able to make observations by, as one might say, rubbing shoulders with them. She saw chimpanzees making implements with which they fished for termites, and twisting up leaves to use as drinking vessels. But, although chimpanzees are capable of making all sorts of useful things, they never seem able to find anywhere to shelter when it rains. Does this not show some incongruity about the statement that, while chimpanzees make and use things but still remain chimpanzees, the same faculty is supposed to have helped hominids to develop into human beings?

Oscar Kiss Maerth, in his book *In the Beginning was the End*, makes the following comment:

A number of scientists have said that standing on their hind legs also helped human beings to run more quickly. Anyone who says that can never have been chased by an angry gorilla. Books would have to be re-written if that ever happened to any of them! Nor do they mention the fact that by walking upright man has sacrificed his ability to climb trees. If he learnt to walk erect because he was afraid of wild animals, he learnt wrong and forgot the real facts. Nowadays he climbs up a tree awkwardly if he happens to meet a wild boar or a lion or a rhinoceros, and would give a great deal to be able to do it more quickly and easily. To lose such abilities at the very time when they were most needed can hardly be called natural development. . . . On this theory, an ape should have developed, who could not find his way back to the remaining forests, who had to look for stones in the long grass, with which – despite his vegetarian habits – he could make an axe to kill a zebra – And it takes a lot of imagination to suppose that all the apes who were to remain apes went back into the woods. . . .

At all events the genus homo sapiens emerged, as anthropologists believe, something like 40,000 years ago, with a brain capacity of about 1,500 cubic centimetres – equivalent to that of present-day man.

The maximum cerebral capacity of his hominid ancestors, on the other hand, was no more than 750 cubic centimetres, hardly greater than that of the gorilla's 685 cubic centimetres. The doubling of the volume of the brain occurred within an amazingly short space of time; compared with the history of evolution, one might say that it happened from one minute to the next; which is all the more remarkable when it is remembered how complex an organ the brain is, and that quality as well as quantity had to be increased; that, moreover, a good many physiological adjustments in the technique of individual communication were necessary. The hominid had suddenly become intelligent and capable of abstract thought – in fact, he had suddenly become human.

In order to explain this apparent miracle, some authors postulate intervention by extra-terrestrial intelligences, who landed on earth in order to manipulate anthropoid apes genetically and transform them into men. Even if, for the sake of argument, this were to be taken as fact, it would not resolve the problem of the awakening of the spirit; it would only transfer it into another dimension.

Much more logical would seem to be the suggestion that the brain power of our hominid ancestors was stimulated by some tremendous shock. Such an experience might have caused changes in the brain.

As early as 1780, Michele Gaetano, the Italian anatomist, showed that the brain is modified by experience. He proved it by experiments on two dogs from the same litter, a pair of goldfinches and two blackbirds, in both cases bred from the same parent birds.

One of each couple was given training over a lengthy period, while the other was left in its natural state. Later on, after they were dead, he examined the brains of all six animals, and discovered that the grey matter of the trained animals contained many more convolutions than that of the untrained. His contemporaries evinced little interest. In 1972, three Americans published the results of lengthy experiments on rats. Mark R. Rosenzweig, Professor of Psychology, L. Bennett, head of the Lawrence Berkeley Laboratory for Chemical Biodynamics, and Marian Cleeves, a Professor of Anatomy, showed quite definitely that even after only one month, the rats' brains had developed noticeable changes, anatomically as well as chemically, as a result of particular experiences.

What event, one might ask, could have stirred our hominid ancestors to so great an extent, that their mental capacity underwent such an immense change from that very moment?

There is one phenomenon that to this day arouses the greatest sense of awe, of fascination, of terror in man — and that is fire. Suppose that, in the dim and distant past a hominid had been playing about with stones one evening, had struck a spark by rubbing two of them together, and some dry twig had caught fire . . . Curiosity might have started off a train of ideas: light – warmth – perhaps danger . . .

Just a chance? Hardly; it was bound to happen sooner or later. And it heralded the moment at which he realized that from then on he would always be able to lighten his darkness by setting fire to dry grass or a chip of wood.

It is very questionable whether man is really only 40,000 years old; for objects made by hand or mechanically have been found embedded in geological formations that are forty *million* years old – an iron nail and a gold thread, for example, from England; a carefully cut metallic die, with precise notches, dating from the tertiary period; and from Nevada comes a real 'footprint in the sands of time' – the impression of a shoe showing even the seam that attached the sole to the upper, found in a vein of coal and back-dated thirteen million years.

So it may be that homo sapiens has turned up over and over again during these millions of years, and has as often vanished. We are never likely to find out just how many splendid, highly-developed civilizations have come and gone in the long course of human history – gone, perhaps, as a result of man's misjudgments.

Possibly we too shall perish before long, suffocated by our own contamination and poisons, buried under what will then be useless technical contrivances, soon to be swallowed up and obliterated by time.

And then, who can tell, somewhere, at some moment, a hominid ape will once more climb down from the trees, will strike a couple of flints together, and again reach for the light.

And if, some day, the new man should at last learn to live by his spirit – he will survive.

13. Visitors from the Future

What you do not understand cannot be yours.
                                                    Goethe

Probably every one of us has at one time or another wondered what the world will look like in the far-off future – what exciting discoveries, what surprises await us.

There has always been someone with the courage to leave a record of his visions of the future – such as Jules Verne, for instance, and other writers of serious science fiction. In most cases, too, their tales have proved not simply to be true, but to err by falling short of the reality – and when they were concerned with technical or scientific matters, words were wanting for detailed descriptions of these visions.

It may be that even a cave man wondered at times what the future would bring; but suppose he had, improbably, been endowed with enough imagination to foresee telescopes, computers, jet planes, transistors, or just a 'simple bicycle', he would, quite obviously, have lacked the vocabulary to explain them to his stone-axe-wielding contemporaries.

Much more probably – supposing that we were able to go back into his time and to ask him his prognosis of the future – he would prophesy a more efficient axe or possibly, if he were quite 'batty' in the eyes of his contemporaries, even some kind of cart.

Assuming that man has enough sense to put the brake on what looks like a reckless career towards race-suicide, who would have the courage even to hazard a guess about what would be possible in, say, five thousand years' time, if science and technology go on developing at the same rate as during the past fifty years?

And if we turn to look into the cosmos, can we be

certain that far wider knowledge does not exist elsewhere? We might remind ourselves that it is not so very long since it was axiomatic that nothing could fly that was heavier than air. And it was stated quite definitely that instant death awaited a man who travelled at a speed greater than thirty-five miles an hour. It seems only like the day before yesterday, too, that eminent scientists were agreed that it was impossible for man to venture into outer space or actually to land on the moon. Who dare say now that travel in time is inconceivable?

In 1949 Dr Kurt Gödel published an interesting article describing the prototype of a universe based on Einstein's general theory of relativity. In this universe it is theoretically possible to travel into any part of the past or the future – on the assumption that matter can be wholly commuted into energy. In addition, a time-machine would have to move at a speed equal to 70.7% of the speed of light, which is to say at least 800 million kilometres per hour. Gödel's theory showed that relativist blue-prints of a world could be made in which the local times of what he called fundamental observers, who are subject to the average course of matter in their environment, cannot be brought into any form of reciprocity that would allow of the creation of a universal time-element.

Closed time-curves exist everywhere according to Gödel's design, that would actually permit an individual to travel into his own past or future.

Obviously Gödel's theory provoked some experts, if only because of the consequences to be expected from taking a trip into one's own past. Unfortunately many of the criticisms were aimed not at logical or mathematical flaws in Gödel's theory, but solely at the fact that it contradicts previous experience.

Yet it is known that tachyons indicate the possibility of time-travel.

Recently a well-known purveyor of popular science put the question: why had no one yet visited us? It would surely be easy enough, he suggested, for the future discoverer of a time-machine to return to the present century – if only as a matter of historical interest.

On 3rd June 1973, *El National*, Venezuela's largest daily newspaper, published the following report:

Mexico City.

The morning was particularly clear and bright.

The radar screens at Benito Juârez airfield showed some flying object in the near neighbourhood. The flight control staff looked up at the sky in astonishment. No one had asked permission to land.

A violet light was approaching at terrific speed, but in no way resembled a jet plane. It circled a complete 360°.

'But no answer was received to a radio challenge; no connection was established,' said Fernando Discua, the control tower supervisor.

With earphones on, the officials waited tensely for some sound or a code-sign.

Nothing.

The unidentified flying object continued circling in a radius of some ten to twelve miles, shrouded in the violet-coloured light. The three officials were startled and anxious. Here was a flying object that showed on their radar screens, that was actually visible to the naked eye, but that gave no reply and made no attempt to land.

At the same time civilian aircraft reported to the control tower over the radio, asking for landing permission and telling them that some unidentifiable round object was flying within sighting distance; it was veiled in phosphorescent light, they said, so that its size could not be determined.

Both Discua's fellow officer Estanol and a third man admitted that they had been panic-stricken when the object appeared on the radar screens but gave no reply whatever to enquiries. 'We were rung up from all over the place, telling us about the UFO to the north of the town. There was no question of its being imagination,' said Estanol. 'The object was moving at an incredible speed and absolutely silently. Then it hung in the air for several seconds, quite motionless, as if it were on the end of a string.'

On the international airfield at Mexico City, the question now is: 'Who was it? When will they be coming back?'

I, Peter Achtmann, attested legal interpreter, aged 34, resident in Berlin, make the following statement:

At about 4.35 in the morning of 18th April 1973, accompanied by two other persons, I was on the western outskirts of Puerto de la Cruz, Tenerife, in the Canary Islands (Spanish). It was still dark, the sky was absolutely cloudless. I was looking north-west. Suddenly I observed two (2) luminous objects flying at the same height but at some distance from one another, travelling at considerable speed in direction from north to south-west. The two objects were of different sizes; for convenience's sake, I concentrated on the larger, left-hand object. In order to ensure that I made no error regarding the movement of the object, I endeavoured to keep my body, and especially my head, as still as possible, and I laid the index finger of my right hand on my eyebrows, parallel with my eyes, so as to limit my angle of vision. The object in question moved well beyond the line of the finger placed upon my completely motionless head.

The object consisted of a more or less clearly recognizable egg-shaped body. At the lower end of this body were two immensely powerful searchlights, that looked like a pair of eyes. They emitted a far-ranging, metallic beam.

Round the body itself were some fifteen or twenty smaller points of light that shone with the same metallic brilliance, so that the whole object looked like a spider with illuminated legs. The light – or, rather, the lights – blazed with unvarying intensity.

I would not care to make a definite statement regarding the distance between my own position and that of the object; but I would surmise that it was at least two (2) miles.

A brief glance at the second object, that is, the one on the right-hand side, revealed an almost identical image, except for the difference in size.

My observations had lasted, I calculate, about two (2) minutes. Then the object on which I had concentrated particularly came to a sudden and complete halt – that is to say, it did not 'hover', as a helicopter would normally do. Both searchlights now moved simultaneously, still shining with the same intensity; the smaller lights too continued to blaze with undiminished brilliance. But after a few moments all the lights went out, and for the fraction of a second the object was surrounded by an odd sort of halo, rather like a magnesium flare. Immediately afterwards, however, it was fully illuminated again, and began to move steeply northwards at tremendous speed. I followed the object with my eyes for about another ten or twelve minutes, in particular the searchlights, as it continued on its northward flight, until I could no longer see it. I have nothing more to add about what happened to the second object.

I am ready at any time to repeat my statement on oath.

Berlin, 20.4.1973.

Peter Achtmann

Africa.

It was one of those quiet, misty mornings, said Antony Fitzgerald (writing to the South African *Aviation News* magazine, Johannesburg), that are typical of the central parts of Natal. The farm manager, Jock Marais, and I were walking down a slope towards the buildings.

Dew dripped from the tall grass. I remember that particularly, because I was wearing an ancient pair of boots, and the sole of one of them had come unstuck. I usually kept them in my twin-engined 'bus, an Aero-

Commander. My feet got soaking wet that morning, and
the thought crossed my mind that relics of this description, even though it may be hard to part with them, can
be of very doubtful value.

A flock of cackling guinea-fowl strutted past us, hunting for food. All of a sudden they stopped dead. Jock
and I noticed it at the same moment.

We looked down from the slope on to the grassy
runway near the house and the hangar. Ndolwana, the
Zulu pilot, had just rolled out the plane in which I was
intending to fly to Durban. It jutted up above the wintry
brown grass in spectral fashion. Suddenly we were aware
of an uncanny glow on the runway, about 300 yards away
from the house. We ourselves were some 200 yards away
from the phenomenon as we came down the path.

In the half-light of dawn I thought at first that it
might be a huge bubble of marsh gas, about forty yards
across. It glowed pink in the centre and faded out towards the circumference, like the manifestations that
pilots call 'sundogs', which sometimes appear between
midnight and dawn.

Involuntarily we slowed down. As the light grew
stronger we noticed that the sheep grazing beside the
runway were ranged in two separate clumps, one on each
side of the bubble, staring at it hypnotically. From where
we were standing, they reminded one of a lot of iron
filings lying on a sheet of paper and being attracted
towards a magnet – a definite image, though with no particular design.

We were still a stone's throw away, when the pink glow
suddenly rose perpendicularly into the air.

Not a sound. Not a breath of wind.

We ran towards the spot, as though under some com-
pulsion. Jock exclaimed: 'Just look at those sheep!' I
had been watching the bubble as it vanished into the
mist, until we reached the spot where it had been. Now
I too noticed in amazement that the sheep were standing
on tiptoe like ballet-dancers, and craning their necks
oddly in an effort to look upwards. Their hoofs seemed

to be almost air-borne, not touching the grass.

We ourselves suddenly felt curiously weightless too. My mouth watered, and the damp in my right boot rose halfway up my leg. To put it mildly, it was an uncanny experience.

Last but not least, Ndolwana added to it all by rushing up to us, his face ashen, shouting, and in a great state of excitement. When he reached us, he gasped breathlessly that he had now, personally, 'really and truly', seen the 'red sun' told of in old Zulu legends. Quite apart from his obvious agitation, this man, the decendant of a Zulu chief, accepted it all as a matter of course.

When asked about it later in an official interrogation, he confirmed that such visitors from another world had been known in Zululand long before any white man had set foot there.

The sheep soon moved about normally again, and we lost the uncomfortable feeling of weightlessness.

I checked over the aircraft before taking off, started the engines as easily as usual and, still deep in thought, taxied along the runway until I was about three hundred yards from where the 'thing' had been. It took a few minutes for the engines to warm up.

Later that day, Jock told me that he had never in all his life seen anything rise so rapidly. As he expressed it, the aircraft was on the runway at one minute, and in the next it was out of sight in the mist.

My own recollection of it is rather confused. The machine rose from the ground like lightning, and within seconds it was in the clouds.

Half stupefied, I groped automatically for the instrument panel. Everything appeared to be normal, except the altimeter and the VSI. The Vertical Speed Indicator was over on the extreme edge, and the altimeter had gone crazy and was whizzing round in circles.

Curiously enough, I had not been forced back into my seat by the tremendous acceleration, so that I did not feel the effect of it in any discomfort. On the contrary,

I found myself sitting much more easily than usual. Almost unconsciously, I pressed the lever for the landing-gear, and was startled at the unusual violence with which it reacted.

As far as I could estimate, I must have been about 10,000 feet up when things returned to normal. I got in touch with Durban by radio, reported the incident, and came down to the prescribed height.

What was it all about?

The selection of possible explanations ranges from lunacy, hallucination and opportunist sensationalism, via nonsense about confusion with balloons, satellites, Venus, and other natural phenomena, to extra-terrestrial space-ships.

Careful investigation of the affair shows very soon that all these suggestions make sense up to a point. Certainly hallucination sometimes plays a part, and for a time the story was quite useful to opportunists. Sects have always existed, so why not a 'Space Brotherhood' for a change, to 'save the human race'?

Of course 'contact men' have turned up too – chosen people, invited to take trips into the empyrean by 'tall, blond, blue-eyed spacemen', and who have returned, bringing occult messages, about which they will only speak oracularly 'lest humanity should come to harm'. And, of course, confusion with aircraft or natural phenomena do actually occur.

But is that really the end of it? A very large proportion of the immense number of sightings is reported by serious, highly qualified, and absolutely reliable observers, such as astronauts, astronomers, pilots, meteorologists, radar experts, police officers, ships' captains, rocket engineers, and responsible people in all walks of life.

Reports about UFOs come from all over the earth; and there is plenty of evidence – in photographs, films, and radar records – to prove the actual existence of these objects. Modern technical methods provide every opportunity for separating the wheat from the chaff; and fakes are easy enough to detect by these means.

For years, groups of UFO enthusiasts have been trying to solve the mystery. But Government departments still refuse to commit themselves; and so secret-mongering continues full blast.

Ingenious publicity has given UFOs such a shady reputation that most people shy off even mentioning them. 'After all,' they say, 'one doesn't want to make a fool of oneself – or to be considered psychopathic!'

The American Air Force at one time found itself obliged by the pressure of public opinion to take the matter seriously. In 1966 Colorado University was commissioned to carry out an enquiry into UFOs. The USAF provided half a million dollars towards the project and appointed Professor E. U. Condon to conduct it. His co-workers were drawn from a wide variety of scientific disciplines. Unfortunately, however, the result of the enquiry was pre-determined – that is to say, it was engaged in from a prejudiced point of view.

Two of Professor Condon's co-workers – Dr Saunders and Dr Levine – who had been recommended beforehand as particularly able, were dropped from the team very soon for alleged incompetence. This was contradicted by a statement that the two scientists owed their dismissal to the fact that they had come to the unbiased and positive conclusion that UFOs really do exist.

Saunders, for example, had prepared several thousand concrete cases for investigation – but the Condon project investigated no more than ninety in all. As an example, the outcome of a single one may be quoted. 'It concerns one of the UFO reports in which all the geometrical, psychological, and physical factors support the view that an unidentified flying object, described as a silvery metallic disc, more than ten yards across, and clearly not of natural origin, was seen by two witnesses.'

Nevertheless, the final report on the Condon Project in 1969 reads: 'There are no proofs to warrant the assumption that extra-terrestrial visitors have entered earth's atmosphere, nor is there sufficient evidence to justify further research into the matter.'

After this, more accusations than ever were made of confusion, superficiality, obviously tendentious methods of research . . . the whole Condon Report, they said, was an absolute scandal and ought to be thoroughly investigated.

Subsequently a study group from the American Institute for Aeronautics and Astronautics – the largest scientific organization in the world for space research – got to work. Eleven scientists and engineers examined the Condon Report under a microscope and reached some amazing conclusions. The expert opinion of the group appeared in November 1970, in the current issue of *Aeronautics and Astrophysics*; it stated that Professor Condon's assertion that it was not worth while to continue scientific investigation into UFOs was totally unfounded. On the contrary, the fact had been established that no more than 30% of all UFO cases had *not* been proved. Furthermore, Professor Condon's view that the earth would not within the next ten thousand years be visited by intelligent beings from beyond the solar system was by no means convincing. In the opinion of the committee, it was impossible to ignore the other well-documented UFO cases; they formed the hard core of the whole controversy, and would have given every reason for carrying on investigations rather than for discontinuing them. Contrary to Condon's statement, a considerable amount of scientific advantage could have been gained from them.

Professor Allen Hynek, the well-known astrophysicist, was for over twenty years scientific adviser to the USAF in the secret UFO project known as the Blue Book. In 1972 he published a very objective work entitled *The UFO Experience – a Scientific Enquiry*, in which he concludes that UFOs really exist.

He recommends . . . 'that in this country (USA) and in others, groups of genuinely interested scientists and engineers should establish an institute for the study of the

UFO problem on a simple but permanent basis . . . Since the phenomenon concerns the *whole of our globe,* contact should be established between members of all countries. Some means of communication would be needed, and an international technical journal concerned with the study of UFO would be advisable . . .

'It would be particularly desirable for a member state of the UN to introduce a proposal to the General Assembly for the establishment of a committee within the UN to promote communication among scientific groups in each country . . .'

In a foot-note, Professor Hynek says that on 18th June 1966 U Thant, then Secretary General of the UN, had expressed to him personally and to the author John Fuller his deep interest in the UFO problem. In the course of a discussion lasting for an hour, the Secretary General had told them that at a meeting of the UN interest had been expressed by members of a number of states. The UN, he said, were in favour of positive action; but obviously this could only be carried out by means of proposals from member nations.

It is clear from all this that Professor Hynek takes UFOs very seriously. And he should know, having been concerned with the matter professionally for over twenty-five years.

Washington, 19th July 1952.

Twenty minutes before midnight, eight UFOs came 'waltzing' into the air space above New York, and were spotted on the radar screens of the civilian air control centre at the National Airport.

A ten-day period of visual and radar-screen sightings followed this first visit. On 29th July, at forty minutes past midnight, seven clearly defined points showed on the radar screens. These foreign bodies moved across the screens at tremendous speed and then, quite suddenly, braked sharply.

Four aircraft pilots, Harry Barnes, Ed Nugent, Jim

Ritchey, and James Copeland, could not believe their eyes. They contacted the control tower and were told by Howard Cocklin, the radio operator there, that the objects were also visible on his screen. 'One of them you can actually see with the naked eye,' he said. 'No idea what they are.' Barnes was not satisfied and called up the Air Force High Command. Then he turned back to his radar screen. Meanwhile the UFOs had broken formation; two were over the White House and one over the Capitol – both prohibited areas.

The foreign bodies had also been observed at the Andrew Field Air Force base, which Barnes contacted. . . .

International headlines, wild confusion, and finally an official démenti followed before public confidence was restored. But this did not solve the problem nor provide satisfactory explanations. Questions came in from every side, even from the office of the President, Harry Truman.

Particular importance was, and is, attached to this episode, because reports were received simultaneously from both eye-witnesses and radar observers. Unknown flying objects were sometimes seen singly and sometimes in groups over New York, on the 19th, 20th, 23rd, 26th, 27th, 28th, and 29th July. They usually showed up between midnight and dawn. The distance flown by UFOs in view of the radar screens was reckoned to be between 100 and 130 miles; which gave their speed on average to be something like 7,200 miles an hour, though from time to time they also flew more slowly. Sightings were reported by civilian aircraft, Air Force pilots and eye-witnesses on the ground. A summary of the observations made by the Air Force showed general agreement that the colours of these UFOs changed from orange to green to red. They did not fly in definite formations.

Finally, the Air Force, yielding to pressure from the public, decided to make a move. On 29th July, Major-General John A. Samford, Head of the Air Force Intelligence Service at the Pentagon, agreed to meet some forty journalists and to answer questions about the UFOs. In order to reassure the general public and to satisfy international curiosity, two points were particularly stressed: Samford said there was no reason to suppose that these objects represented any threat to the United States. And second, an attempt was made to explain away the whole affair as a natural phenomenon, despite the fact that various proofs, including photographs, existed to prove the contrary. Experts have never been satisfied with this very lame explanation ...

Portugal, 4th September 1957.

At 19.21 hours, four jet fighters took off from the military base of Ota for a navigational night flight. It was a routine exercise, to be carried out via Granada, in Spain, and back over the Portuguese towns of Portalegre and Coruche, flying at 8,000 metres. Flight Captain Jose Lemos Ferreira was in charge of the operation, with three other pilots accompanying him. The night was clear and starry.

The first part of the exercise proceeded smoothly and according to plan. From Granada the aircraft turned off in the direction of Portalegre.

At this point Captain Ferreira noticed an unusually bright light to port, on the horizon. He watched it for a few minutes, and then alerted the other pilots over the radio. The pilot on the left wing had already seen it.

Something at the heart of the curious glow changed colour continuously from dark green to blue, yellow and red. Suddenly it increased to five or six times its original size. And before the pilots had time to take this in, it had shrunk to an almost invisible yellow dot. This was repeated several times over.

While all this was going on, it never changed its position relative to the aircraft, remaining at an angle of about 40° to port. Captain Ferreira was unable to see how the changes in size came about, whether while the object was in motion or when it was stationary. After six or seven minutes of constant variations in size, it vanished over the horizon at an angle of about 90° to the left of the jets.

At 22.38 hours, shortly before reaching Portalegre, the

captain decided to make for Coruche, and the formation veered about 50° to port; lo and behold the UFO was there again, still at an angle of 90° to the aircraft. This convinced Captain Ferreira that it could not be stationary. Meanwhile it shone bright red and lay well below the altitude of the Air Force machines.

After the pilots had been on the new course for some minutes, they suddenly saw a smaller flying object detaching from the large one. They had hardly recovered from their surprise, when three more of these little objects appeared to the right of the large UFO. It moved continuously at varying speeds, with its small companions always in the same relative position.

Yet, despite the fact that the UFOs were fairly near, and flying far below the jets, it was impossible to judge exactly the distance between them. The large UFO was about fifteen times the size of the smaller ones, and appeared to be in command, as the smaller ones formed up around it.

As the Air Force machines approached Coruche, the large UFO suddenly nose-dived violently and immediately rose again at the same speed, but heading towards the jets. The pilots were beside themselves and almost broke formation in order to climb laterally above the UFO; but as soon as they cut across its path, the UFO and its companions retreated.

The incident had lasted about forty minutes, and all the pilots were agreed that no natural explanation was possible.

Captain Ferreira said that he hoped and prayed not to be fobbed off with the routine explanations about its being Venus, balloons, aircraft, or some such things, as had become the practice whenever a UFO was sighted.

One particular characteristic has always been noted when UFOs do appear: 'They seem to come up out of the void, like a light being switched on!' After they appear they are described as solid metallic objects that seem to dissolve into 'nothing' when they vanish (transformed into energy). Just as they emerge 'out of the blue', so they fade out, and the typical description is that 'it went out like a light being switched off'.

It is worth noting that these would be the very characteristics to be found in a time machine. For a time machine must necessarily have the capacity to transform itself into energy – to dematerialize so to speak. For this reason, one might well wonder whether some UFOs are time machines that might not necessarily be coming from some other planetary system, but might indeed be terrestrial time machines of the future.

'If so, why don't they land, and make contact with us?' is the ever-recurrent question. Responsibility for this might lie in certain definite physical laws that would prevent such machines and their occupants from landing and making contact. Or there might possibly be sociological reasons.

There have, it is true, been thousands of reports of alleged landings, but such stories must always be treated with considerable caution. Hoaxers and unreliable witnesses have already done much harm. Nevertheless, the following case is worth noting, for it is said to be authentic and no contradictions have been substantiated.

1st July 1965, Valensole, Basses Alpes, France.

All through the month of June, M. Maurice Masse and his father, market gardeners in Valensole, had with mounting fury noticed that someone had been stealing young plants from l'Olivol, their lavender field.

Early in the morning of 1st July, at about 5.45, Maurice Masse stubbed out a cigarette and prepared to carry on with his work. He was standing beside a pile of gravel at the end of a small vineyard that bordered on the lavender field.

Suddenly he heard a whistling noise. He looked round casually, thinking it was a helicopter. He was more than startled to see instead a globular 'machine' that was about the size of a Dauphine car. It stood on six landing props and a central pivot. Beside it were two figures stooping over the lavender plants. Raging, Masse watched them through the vines. Then he left his cover and ran towards the two strangers. When he got to within about 15 metres of them, one turned and pointed something that looked like a pencil at him. Masse stood rooted to the spot, incapable of moving.

Telling the story later, Masse described the creatures as being 1.20 metres (a little under 5 feet) in height, wearing close-fitting one-piece garments. He had nothing whatever to say about anything else that might have happened during the encounter.

After they had returned to their machine a short time later, Masse saw that they were watching him from the interior. The landing gear was retracted, there was a dull thud from the central pivot, and the machine rose soundlessly off the ground. When it had gone about 25 metres, it suddenly became invisible, although tracks were left on the ground that seemed to point towards Manosque. The local police were immediately alerted and came to make enquiries. They saw the marks made in the ground by the landing gear.

M. Masse is regarded by the neighbours as a reliable sort of man, with plenty of sound common sense.

England, late August/early September 1968.

At half past ten o'clock one evening, George Graham, a farmer, was as usual standing patiently at the edge of the woodland with a gun in his hand, watching for foxes. His attention was suddenly attracted by an odd light about a hundred yards ahead of him in the middle of a field.

'At first I thought it was one of the farmers tinkering with a lorry, so I took no particular notice,' said the seventy-five-year-old owner of a farm in the village of Woodmanstone near Banstead, in Surrey.

'All of a sudden I heard a sort of "whoosh" – I can't describe it in any other way. I turned to look down the field again and could just see the outlines of a dark shape that rose into the air without a sound. It put on speed and in a few seconds it had vanished in the darkness.'

On the following day Mr Graham searched the field, in case he might find anything that would give him a lead towards identifying the nocturnal visitor.

He did in fact find a mark that he described as a depression in the ground, 'like an enormous horseshoe with a tail to it, about fifty yards long and twenty-five wide'. The outer edges seemed as if they had been cut sharply into the soil by something like a vacuum cleaner, throwing up the earth for eight or ten inches all round. 'I think someone from "the beyond" was trying an experiment,' suggested the old farmer. 'Anyhow, it was a huge great thing, at least as big as a double-decker 'bus. However could "they" get it up into the air so quietly?' Mr Graham wondered.

Many people confronted by a UFO have said afterwards that they felt they were being closely observed from the interior of the object.

If the time-travel theory is correct, and there are time-travellers in UFOs, then it would be only natural that they should wish to observe us closely.

Australia, 31st October 1967, 9 p.m.

Mr Spargo, a contractor, got into his car to go from Konjonup to Boyup Brook. He had just paid off one of his sheep-shearing 'teams and was intending to take the week's wages to his people at Boyup Brook.

There was little traffic on the road and the sky was bright with stars. Some twelve miles off Boyup Brook the car stopped abruptly. The light went off and so did the radio – the electricity had failed. Mr Spargo was beside himself with annoyance. He could not understand why the car had simply stopped with a jerk when, a moment before, it had been bowling along the road at sixty miles an hour, with no sign of any defect and without his having braked.

He could not think what to do; nor did there seem to be any explanation. If you apply the brakes suddenly while travelling at sixty miles an hour, you are catapulted forward. But all that had happened was that he had stopped and did not know why. All he did know was that he was in the focus of a brilliant beam of light, in the middle of hilly country, in which occasional trees reared their heads sixty feet into the sky.

Then he saw that the light-ray proceeded from a mushroom-shaped object with a diameter of about twelve feet and surrounded by blazing light, that floated over the tops of the trees, about fifty feet from the ground. The ray directed at him came from a tube projecting through the bottom of the flying object at an angle of about 45°.

To the psychiatrist Dr Paul Zeck, who later questioned him closely about the whole affair, he said: 'I don't know how far away from me this tube was; I felt as if I were somehow enclosed in it. Its diameter was about three feet and it was shiny outside. I could look inside it, but there was nothing to see, not even any light. My eyes didn't hurt. I rather had the feeling that the inside of my car was lit up by it, but I did not look round.

'I felt that I was being watched through that tube. But I couldn't distinguish anything except the outlines of the object. I simply *had* to look into the tube. Why? No idea. As far as I can remember, I wasn't thinking of anything at all. I felt no fear. I just sat there, staring into this tube.

'After five minutes or thereabouts it went out, like a light being switched off. The colour of the object seemed to grow darker, it got up speed suddenly and vanished westwards at a terrific rate. It was out of sight within a couple of seconds.'

There was another surprise in store for Mr Spargo – he found that he was moving again. He had no more idea of how he had restarted than he had of why he had stopped. Now he halted quite voluntarily at the side of the road, got out of the car and searched the sky. Nothing was to be seen except the stars. He got back into the car and went on towards Boyup Brook. His first call there was to the local police station, where he reported the incident. As he saw it, it was essential for the authorities to be informed, but he requested that his name should be kept out of the newspapers.

When Dr Zeck asked whether he could remember any sounds, Mr Spargo realized, to his surprise, that he heard absolutely nothing. 'Odd,' he said, 'usually if you halt in the bush at night, you hear frogs croaking, grasshoppers chirping, and all sorts of noises.'

The whole episode must have lasted about five minutes. When he reached Boyup Brook, Mr Spargo saw that his wrist-watch – which was usually accurate to a second – was five minutes slow. It must have stopped when he halted in the bush.

The sighting was reported in *The West Australian* on 1st November 1967. Besides Mr Spargo, numbers of other witnesses among farmers and sheep-shearers had seen it.

The idea that UFOs are a modern phenomenon and were invented in order to provide some sort of compensatory religion in a repressive, impersonal, technological world, is absolutely false. UFOs have been recorded since the dawn of human existence.

If, as we have assumed, UFOs are time machines, then they at least refute the argument which says that time-travellers cannot take part in past events or that they might actually change them. Even if UFOs do not make direct contact with us, they alter the course of history simply by allowing us to see them.

By the very fact of their appearance, they caused at least one new event – they activated the Condon Report. So one must agree that UFOs, in their capacity as time machines, do take part in history and influence it in a number of ways.

The oldest records of flying objects are probably those discovered on rock carvings. Many of these go back 20,000 years, and have been discovered in Spain, France, South America and elsewhere.

In a 12,000-year-old Brazilian cave near Varzelandia, flying objects are depicted that quite definitely resemble modern descriptions of UFOs. In addition, marvellous to relate, a picture of our solar system, drawn to scale, was discovered in the same cave.

Myths, fables, traditions, religions, all tell of flying objects. Moreover, stories dating from the Middle Ages and from the beginning of modern times also tell of such phenomena.

During the night of 1st January 1254, for example, monks in St Alban's Abbey in England saw something in the heavens that looked like a ship, in glorious colours (*Historia Anglorum*).

As the Abbot of Durham was being carried to his burial in 1320, a great light appeared in the sky, and seemed to shine over the place where he was to be interred. Later it was observed to be gliding downwards, moving from one spot to another (*Historia de Statu Ecclesiae Dunelmensis*).

On 9th July 1698, the German astronomer Gottfried Kirch reported from Leipzig that he had at 1.30 in the morning watched a fiery globe with a long tail, that had risen at an angle of about $8\frac{1}{2}°$ from Aquarius, and had remained in that position for one-eighth of an hour without moving. He judged its diameter to have been roughly half that of the moon. At first its light had been so bright that it was possible to read without using a candle; but then it had gradually faded, and had finally disappeared completely. Other people, too, including Schlazius, who lived about fifteen kilometres from Leipzig, had seen the object at the same time.

On 17th June 1777, the French astronomer Messier sighted a number of round dark objects in the sky.

France.

In 1790 an Inspector of Police named Liabeuf was sent from Paris to Alençon to investigate a curious occurrence. He reported as follows:

On 12th June at five o'clock in the morning, some peasants watched an enormous 'globe' that appeared to be surrounded by flames. At first they thought it was a Montgolfier balloon that had caught fire; but they were astonished at the great speed with which it was travelling, and the whistling noise it made. Then the globe slowed down, swayed slightly, and crash-landed on top of a hillock, rooting up all the vegetation. The heat emitted by the object was so intense that grass and bushes burst into flames.

The peasants succeeded in containing the fire, which would otherwise have destroyed things all round. By evening, the 'globe' was still hot. And then a very odd – almost incredible – event occurred. Eye-witnesses were two mayors, a doctor, and three other local notables, who will confirm my story, not forgetting the dozen or so peasants who were present.

The news had spread rapidly and curiosity brought people from every direction.

The sphere, which was large enough to hold a cart, was completely intact, despite its crash.

Suddenly a kind of door opened in the machine, and – this is the interesting part of the story – an individual emerged, someone who looked just like ourselves except that he was dressed differently. He was wearing a single, close-fitting garment. Upon seeing the crowd of people, this man muttered something and ran into the woodland.

The peasants drew back instinctively, nervously – and that saved their lives, because, a few moments later, the object exploded without a sound; the wreckage flew in all directions, and finally disintegrated into a sort of powder.

Search made for the mysterious man produced no result; he seemed to have vanished into thin air, and not the smallest trace of him was ever found. It was as if he had gone out of our world, leaving nothing behind.

Could it have been someone from another world? I am no scholar, but the idea suddenly came into my mind . . .

An account of the episode was sent immediately to the French Academy of Sciences, and was received by its eminent members with appropriate sarcasm. They declared with absolute certainty that it was impossible for any living being to come to earth in such a fashion. They refused even to inspect the hole that had been made by the explosion and which remained visible for years.

(Alberto Fengolio, *Clypeus* Anno III No. 3)

An unrecognizable shoal of curious objects was seen by a number of people during an eclipse of the moon on 7th September 1820. These objects moved in an absolutely straight line, flew over the city of Embrun in France, performed a 90° turn without breaking formation and proceeded on their new course.

(Francis Arago, *Annales de chimie et physique*)

On 20th August 1880, Monsieur Trecul, a member of the French Academy, observed a glittering, white-gold, cigar-shaped flying object, with pointed ends. He also saw a small round object detaching from the larger one.

On 12th August 1883, Señor Bouilla, astronomer at the Zacatecas Observatory in Mexico, sighted a large number of circular flying objects silhouetted against the sun.

An aircraft that nobody could identify, showing bluish-green and white lights, appeared over Kansas City, Missouri, in April 1897. Ten thousand people saw it as it hovered above the city for ten minutes before shooting off rapidly upwards. At the same time similar UFOs were observed over several others of the United States.

In 1905, a glowing disc, surrounded by a halo of rays, was seen over Cherbourg in France on several consecutive nights.

At 11 o'clock at night on 31st July 1916, a bright object was seen in the sky over Ballinasloe, Ireland. It was visible for fifteen minutes before it moved off in a north-westerly direction.

(*The Books of Charles Fort*)

One August morning in the middle 1920s, while the well-known explorer Nicholas Roerich and members of his expedition were on their way to Mongolia, they saw a gigantic egg-shaped object moving in the sky at great speed. Its smooth upper surface reflected the sunlight dazzlingly on one side. Roerich and his companions watched the manoeuvres of the aircraft through their field glasses.

On 26th February 1942, the cruiser *Van Tromp* of the Royal Netherlands Navy was in the Timor Sea. Suddenly a large aluminium disc approached the Dutch ship and circled above it at a great height for three or four hours. Eventually it shot off at the rate of between 4,500 and 5,300 kilometres an hour. The duty officer was unable to identify the object.

On Sunday, 10th September 1967, at 11 o'clock in the morning, a DC6 of the Air Ferry Lines spotted an un-identified flying object. The DC6 was flying between Mallorca and Manston (England) at 16,000 feet, and was sixty-five miles north of Reus in North-East Spain.

The sun was shining but there was slight mist. All at once Captain Underhill noticed a 'black patch' about sixty miles ahead that, according to the pilot's calculation, changed its position from port to starboard at supersonic speed. When the object came more or less in line with the aircraft, it appeared to decrease speed, and gave the impression of being cigar-shaped.

Captain Underhill surmised that there was a formation of aircraft, and discussed it with his co-pilot; at the same time he called in the flight engineer Brian Dunlop. At this moment the object turned towards the DC6 with still further decreased speed. And Underhill summoned the steward as an additional witness. As the latter stepped into the cockpit, the outlines of the object assumed conical form. It shone silvery above and sloped away in a curve below; it was evidently metallic and gave the impression of being solid, or very nearly solid. It flew past the DC6, about half a mile below it, leaving no trace whatever, and was in sight for about two and a half minutes.

'It was certainly not a balloon nor any kind of unfamiliar aircraft,' the four witnesses stated categorically when they reported the incident.

Spanish control stations were alerted, but showed only slight interest. The RAF station at Manston, on the other hand, was very much interested in Captain Underhill's report.

(*The Daily Express*, London, 11th September 1967)

Now that man has once again taken a first step towards venturing into space, some astronauts have also reported UFO sightings.

In view of the tremendous amount of evidence about UFOs, it looks like self-delusion simply to dismiss them as crack-brained nonsense, or to ridicule the whole idea, as tends to be the fashion.

We shall have to accustom ourselves to the fact that flying objects, of unknown origin but seemingly controlled by intelligent beings, really are appearing in our air space.

14. Adventure in Time

Whether you speak truth or tell a lie is immaterial.
Either will be contradicted.

Goethe

We have travelled only a very short way along one of the many roads in the realm of Time. As we went, we had some curious encounters; but these are the very things that show how little we know as yet about time, consciousness, and life in general.

Even if we cannot accept as valid all we are told, we must still agree that possibilities await us that may yet turn our lives in the cosmos into an exciting adventure. For it looks as though our physical existence may be no more than a single aspect of life as a whole. And if we assume that there is a universal creative force of which we are a part, then this force shows its enormous wealth of inspiration, if only by allowing us to know and to use the material side of nature also.

Actually, exploration of matter has hardly begun yet, but everything goes to show that humanity has at its disposal immense potentials of science and technology, so long as they are used with discretion.

All the same, it seems short-sighted to concentrate on this aspect alone. For undreamed-of possibilities are also awaiting us in the sphere of the mind. The very fact that the mind is able to project itself into the past and the future – as experiments show clearly – reveals perspectives that man has hitherto failed to exploit.

Restrictions imposed upon us by the limitations of the material world of science and technology do not exist in the unfathomed domains where neither distance nor speed, yesterday and today, before or after, have any significance.

One of the greatest adventures awaiting humanity is

the exploration of the cosmos in the search for other forms of life. If we are to succeed, the problem of times and space will have to be solved.

One road to the stars would be the systematic cultivation of the extra-sensory faculties. Further development of telepathy, telekinesis and mind-projection might, *inter alia*, lead to communication with other intelligences.

Intensive study of man's 'second nature' would no doubt also throw light upon the mystery of death – might show whether there really is a life after death.

If we were to discover – and there are many signs pointing in this direction – that our physical existence is indeed only a short interval in another, more permanent spiritual life, our ideology would need to undergo a complete and drastic change.

It should not really surprise us to find a personality, an 'I am', after death. For would that not be altogether the most appropriate rationale for the existence of a universe? Certainly it would explain a great many of the phenomena that have been discussed in this book; phenomena that also show that we are capable of acting on two levels in time – on a metaphysical, parapsychological level as well as on the physical and technological plane.

Re-incarnation alone would to a limited extent turn us into time-travellers. And there appear to be definite signs that certain notable personalities have in the course of history made full use of time-travel.

Saint-Germain is one of these. Do people such as he come from the future? How else could his mysterious description of a cosmic journey and his detailed information about inventions made after his day be explained?

Wheeler's super-space or parallel universe, verification of tachyons, of Gödel's space-time hypothesis, and the discovery of fresh aspects in science and technology, point to another and equally exciting kind of time-travel. And that too would be a road to the stars.

In the infinity of time and space there must undoubtedly be civilizations that are already making full use of these possibilities; so belief in the appearance of extra-terrestrial visitors now or in the past cannot be shrugged off as non-sense.

The fact that biological signals from living beings in a distant planetary system, as well as echo-signals from a possibly extra-terrestrial space-probe have been recorded, show that visitors from 'outside' appear also to be interested in making contact with us.

The seriousness with which the theory about the sonde of Epsilon Boötes is taken, is shown by the fact that the sky-lab astronauts have been told to look out for it.

And, finally, the value of UFO phenomena should not be under-rated. They might well show that extra-terrestrial intelligences are holding out a hand towards Earth.

The arrogant and egocentric view that we 'earthlings' are unique in the cosmos lacks all foundation in the light of our most recent knowledge. Biochemistry has shown that wherever certain conditions exist, life will eventually evolve. Life in its turn develops intelligence, in order to control its environment. So our world may be regarded as a stepping-stone to start us off on exploratory journeys into other worlds.

'I still remember,' said astronaut Neil Armstrong, 'how I suddenly realized on the way home in Apollo XI, that that tiny, pretty little blue pea was the earth. I held up my thumb and shut one eye – and my thumb blotted out the earth. I did not feel like a giant. I felt very, very small.'

Unfortunately, man is indeed in a position nowadays to blot out that pretty little blue pea – his space-craft Earth – with his thumb. For, to balance his increasing powers, he has not developed a corresponding feeling of respon-sibility.

In an article appearing in *Die Naturwissenschaften* (The Natural Sciences) in June 1973 under the title *Grenzen des Wachstums* (Limits of Growth), C. F. von Weizsäcker says:

'The immediate and acute problems arising from the wastage of resources and the spread of pollution, in addi-tion to that of providing for the needs of an unrestricted increase in world population, are serious enough to require radical and drastic measures . . . At the present time environmental problems still appear to be capable of solution, but only by the exercise of a very great deal of good sense and good will.'

And, years ago, Bertrand Russell wrote:

'The world needs wisdom as it never needed it before. If man should attain it, his new power over nature would offer him prospects of happiness and well-being such as he has never experienced and could probably hardly imagine. – But if he fails to attain it, every increase in skill will only throw him further into irreparable misery. Humanity has done much good and much evil. Many of the good things were very good. All those who value the good, must hope with their whole hearts that at this decisive moment a wise choice may be made.'

In which direction will such a step be taken?

Will it be rectograde or will it be an advance into a better future . . .?

Bibliography

Ägyptisches Totenbuch. Otto Wilhelm Barth Verlag, Weilheim Obb., 1970.

Alfvén, H.: *Kosmologie und Antimaterie*. Umschau Verlag Frankfurt/Main 1969.

Ambarzumjan, V.: 'Die Tiefen der Galaxien'. *Bild der Wissenschaft*, Dec. 1971.

Asimov, I.: 'The Ultimate Speed Limit'. *Saturday Review*, July 1972.

Aurobindo, Sri: *Die Synthese des Yoga*. Verlag Hinder & Deelmann 1972.

Ayer, A. J.: *The Problem of Knowledge*. Penguin Books, Harmondsworth 1961.

Ball, Sir Robert Stawell: *The Story of the Heavens*. Cassell & Company Ltd, London, Paris, Melbourne 1890.

Bond, A.: 'Problems of Interstellar Propulsion'. *Spaceflight*, July 1971, The British Interplanetary Society.

Bondi, H.; Bonner, W. B.; Whitrow, G. J.: *Rival Theories of Cosmology*. Oxford University Press 1960.

Brouwer, D.; Clemence, G. M.: *Methods of Celestial Mechanics*. Academy Press, New York, London 1961.

Buttlar, J. v.: *Schneller als das Licht*. Econ Verlag, Düsseldorf/Wien 1972.

Cerminara, G.: *Many Mansions*. Neville Spearman, London 1971.

Charon, J.: *Cosmology*. World University Library 1970.

Camp van de, P.: *Planetary Companions of Stars*. Pergamon Press 1956.

CETI Questionnaire. *Spaceflight*, April 1973, The British Interplanetary Society, London.

Condon, E. U.: *Scientific Study of unidentified flying objects*. Bantam Book, by arrangement with the University of Colorado 1969.

Cordan, W.: *Das Buch des Rates, Mythos und Geschichte der Maya*, Diederichs, 1962.

Drake, F. D.: 'Project Ozma'. *Physics Today*, Bd. 14 April 1961

Drake, F. D.: *Intelligent Life in Space*. Macmillan, London 1962.

Drake, R. W.: 'Spacemen in the Middle Ages'. *Flying Saucer Review*, London, May/June 1964.

Dunne, J. W.: *An Experiment with Time*. Faber & Faber Ltd, London 1927.

Einstein, A.: *Grundzüge der Relativitätstheorie*. Vieweg 1963.

Einstein, A.: *Ann. Physik*, 17, 1905.

Einstein, A.: *Mein Weltbild*. Amsterdam 1934.

Eliade, M.: *Schamanismus und archaische Ekstasetechnik*. Rascher Verlag, Zürich/Stuttgart.

Eliade, M.: *Yoga, Unsterblichkeit und Freiheit*. Rascher Verlag, Zürich/Stuttgart 1960.

Eliade, M.: *Das Mysterium der Wiedergeburt*. Rascher Verlag, Zürich/Stuttgart 1961.

Flying Saucer Review: Case Histories, February 1971.

Ford, A.: *Bericht vom Leben nach dem Tode*. Scherz, Bern, München, Wien.

Foster, G. V.: 'Non-Human Artifacts in the Solar System'. *Spaceflight*, December 1972, The British Interplanetary Society.

Foss, B. M.: *New Horizons in Psychology*. Penguin Books, Harmondsworth 1966.

Fowler, W. A. and Hoyle, F.: *Nucleosynthesis in massive Stars and Supernovae*. The University of Chicago Press 1964.

Fox, S. W.: 'Chemical Origins of Cells'. *Chemical & Engineering News*, December 1971.

Freud, S.: *Totem and Taboo*. Routledge & Kegan Paul, London 1960.

Freud, S.: *Two short accounts of Psycho-Analysis*. Penguin Books, Harmondsworth.

Freud, S.: *The Interpretation of Dreams*, revised ed. London 1932.

Fulcanelli: *Le Mystère des Cathédrales*. Neville Spearman, London 1972.

Gallenkamp, Ch.: *Maya, The Worlds of Sciences*. Pyramid Publications Inc., New York 1959.

Gamow, G.: *Matter, Earth and Sky*. Macmillan & Co., London 1960.

Gilgamesh Epos. Reclam 1966.

Glob, P. V.: *Die Schläfer im Moor*. Winkler Verlag, München 1966.

Goodall-Lawick van, J.: *Wilde Schimpansen*. Rowohlt, Hamburg 1971.

Govinda, A. Lama: *Grundlagen tibetischer Mystik*. Rascher Verlag, Zürich/Stuttgart 1956.

Govinda, A. Lama: *Der Weg der weissen Wolken*. Rascher Verlag, Zürich/Stuttgart 1966.

'Greening of the Astronauts, The'. *Time*, December 1972.

Grüsser, O.-J.: 'Informationstheorie und die Signalverarbeitung in den Sinnesorganen und im Nervensystem'. *Die Naturwisseschaften,* Springer Verlag, Berlin, Heidelberg, New York, October 1972.

Guirdham, A.: *The Cathars and Reincarnation.* Neville Spearman, London 1970.

Heath, Sir Th.: *Aristarchus of Samos, the Ancient Copernicus.* Clarendon Press, Oxford 1913.

Hoyle, F.: *Galaxies, Nuclei and Quasars.* Heinemann, London 1966.

Hoyle, F.: *Frontiers of Astronomy.* Mercury Books, London 1963.

Huang, Su-Shu: 'Occurrence of Life in the Universe'. *American Scientist,* 47, Nr. 3, 1959.

Hynek, J. A.: *The UFO Experience, a Scientific Inquiry.* Henry Regnery Company, Chicago 1972.

Interstellar Communications Signals. Ecola Institute 1972.

'Is there Life on Mars or beyond?' *Time,* December 1972.

Jacobson, N.-O.: *Leben nach dem Tod?* Sven Erik Bergh im Econ Verlag, Düsseldorf, Wien 1972.

Joachim, J.: 'Plants—The Key to mental Telepathy?' *Probe-Magazine,* December 1972.

Jungk, R.: 'Hilfe aus dem All?' *X-Magazine,* December 1972.

Katchalsky, A.: 'Prebiotic Synthesis of Biopolymers on Inorganic Templates'. *Die Naturwissenschaften,* May 1973, Springer Verlag, Berlin, Heidelberg, New York.

Klingmüller, W.: 'Genkonversion'. *Die Naturwissenschaften,* February 1973, Springer Verlag, Berlin, Heidelberg, New York.

Kompanejez, A.: 'Quantenspiel der Gedankenfreiheit'. *Bild der Wissenschaft,* DVA September 1972.

Kramer, S. N.: *Geschichte beginnt mit Sumer.* List 1959.

Lao-Tse: *Tao-teh-King.* Baum-Verlag, Pfullingen/Württ, 1961.

Lawrence, L. G.: 'Electronics and the living Plant'. *Electronics World,* October 1969.

Lucretius: *The Nature of the Universe.* Penguin Books, Harmondsworth.

Lunan, D. A.: 'Space Probe from Epsilon Boötes'. *Spaceflight,* April 1973, The British Interplanetary Society.

Maerth, O. K.: *Der Anfang war das Ende,* Econ Verlag, Düsseldorf, Wien 1971.

Marcuse, F. L.: *Hypnosis Fact and Fiction.* Penguin Books, Harmondsworth 1963.

Meadows, D.: *Die Grenzen des Wachstums.* Deutsche Verlags-Anstalt Stuttgart 1972.

Mijovic, P.: *Decani, Medieval Art in Yugoslavia.* Publishing House Jugoslavija, Beograd 1966.

Monod, J.: *Le Hasard et la Necessité*, Paris 1971.

Monroe, R. A.: *Der Mann mit den zwei Leben*. Econ Verlag, Düsseldorf, Wien 1972.

Monthly Notices of the Royal Astronomical Society 1971–73, London.

Morgan, J. W.: 'Superrelativistic Interstellar Flight'. *Spaceflight*, July 1973, The British Interplanetary Society.

Munitz, M. K.: *Theories of the Universe from Babylonian Myth to modern Science*. The Free Press 1957.

Negowskij: *Reanimation*. Econ Verlag Düsseldorf, Wien 1969.

'New worlds revealed by living transducers?' *Electrical Review*, London, June 1972.

Nielsen, E.: *Das grosse Geheimnis*. Wilhelm Langewiesche-Brandt, Ebenhausen.

O'Neill, J. J.: *Prodigil Genius, The Life of Nikola Tesla*. Neville Spearman, London 1968.

Oparin, A. J.: *The Origin of Life on Earth*. Academic Press 1957.

Oparin, A. J.: *Origin of Life*. Dover Publications, New York 1953.

Ordway III., F. L.: *Advances in Space Science and Technology*. Academic Press, New York/London 1966.

Ostrander/Shroeder: *PPI*. Scherz Verlag, Bern, München, Wien 1971.

Oswald, I.: *Sleep*. Penguin Books, Harmondsworth 1966.

Ouspensky, P. D.: *In Search of the Miraculous*. Routledge & Kegan Paul, London 1950.

Pauwels, L.; Bergier, J.: *Eternal Man*. Souvenir Press, London 1972.

Pilbeam, D. R.: 'Man's earliest Ancestors'. *Science Journal*, Vol. 3, No. 2, February 1967.

Powell, C.: 'Interstellar Flight and Intelligence in the Universe'. *Spaceflight*, Dec. 1972, The British Interplanetary Society.

Prel du, C.: *Das Rätsel des Menschen*. R. Lönit, Wiesbaden.

Prokoshkin, Yu. D.: 'Particles of Antimatter'. *Die Naturwissenschaften*, July 1972, Springer Verlag, Berlin, Heidelberg, New York.

Rapaport, D.: *Emotions and Memory*. Science Editions, Inc., New York 1961.

Rhine, J. B.: *The Reach of the Mind*. Faber, London 1948.

Ringger, P.: *Parapsychologie, die Wissenschaft des Okkulten*. Werner Classen Verlag, Zürich 1957.

Rosenfeld, A.: *Die zweite Schöpfung*. Econ Verlag, Düsseldorf, Wien 1970.

Rosenzweig, R.; Bennett, E. L.; Diamond, M. C.: 'Brain Changes in Response to Experience'. *Scientific American*, February 1972.

Ruppelt, E. J.: *The Report on Unidentified Flying Objects*. Garden City, New York 1956.

Russell, Bertrand: *The Expanding Mental Universe—Adventures of the Mind*. Victor Gollancz Ltd, London 1960.

Shapley, H.: *Of Stars and Men*. Beacon Press, Boston 1958.

Smith, F. G.: *Radio Astronomy*. Penguin Books, Harmondsworth 1966.

Sudre, R.: *Treatise on Parapsychology*. Allen and Unwin, London 1956.

Schmegler, H.: 'Schneller als Licht'. *Bild der Wissenschaft*, DVA, April 1972.

Schrödter, W.: *Neuer Ausflug ins Wundersame*. Verlag Hermann Bauer KG, Freiburg i. B. 1967.

Starship Study: 'Progress Report'. *Spaceflight*, June 1973, The British Interplanetary Society.

Stearn, J.: *Geheimnisse aus der Welt der Psyche*. Ramòn F. Keller Verlag, Genf 1972.

Struve, O.: *Stellar Evolution*. Princeton University Press 1950.

Tabori, P.; Raphael, Ph.: *Signale aus dem Unbekannten*. H. M. Hieronimi Verlag, Bonn 1972.

Taylor, E. F.; Wheeler, J. A.: *Spacetime Physics*. W. H. Freeman & Co., San Francisco/London 1966.

Teilhard de Chardin, P.: *The Phenomenon of Man*. Fontana Books 1959.

Tibetanische Totenbuch, das. Walter Verlag Olten/Freiburg i. Br. 1971.

Tompkins, P. and Bird, C.: 'Love among the Cabbages'. *Harper's Magazine*, November 1972.

Turner, B. E.: 'Interstellar Molecules'. *Scientific American*, March 1973.

'Turning point in Life'. *Spaceflight*, Volume 14, No. 11, 1972, The British Interplanetary Society.

Tweedale, Ch. L.: *Man's Survival after Death*. Spiritualist Press, London 1909.

UFO Nachrichten, Wiesbaden, June/July 1973.

Ulrici, W.; Nahm, W.: 'Eine neue Gravitationstheorie', Umschau 1969, Heft 8.

Visuddhi-Magga. Verlag Christiani, Konstanz 1952.

Walter Grey, W.: *The Living Brain*. Penguin Books, Harmondsworth 1961.

Was ist der Tod? R. Piper & Co., Verlag München 1969.

Watson, J. D.: *The Double Helix*. The New American Library, Signet 1969.

Weidemann, V.: 'Relativistische Astrophysik'. *Die Naturwissen-*

schaften, April 1973, Springer Verlag, Berlin, Heidelberg, New York.

Weizäcker von C. F.: 'Grenzen des Washstums'. *Die Naturwissen-schaften*, June 1973, Springer Verlag, Berlin, Heidelberg, New York.

Wells, H. G.: *The Time Machine*, Pan Books Ltd, London 1969.

West, D. J.: *Psychical Research Today*. Penguin Books, Harmondsworth 1962.

Wood, E.: *Grundriss der Yogalehre*. Hans E. Günther Verlag, Stuttgart 1961.

Index of Names

Subject Index